Self-Analysis By the Stars

ASTROLOGY: YOUR PERSONAL SUN-SIGN GUIDE

By Beatrice Ryder

Foreword by Birdfeather

Do you want to know how to increase your glamor? Find out how the stars influence normal and abnormal sex tendencies? Which music will soothe your soul? Which planets affect your pet's health?

This exciting new astrology book is unique in that it requires no calculations, and is designed to delineate the character and provide readings without charts, pencil work or mathematics. The work is based on Sun-Sign and Decanate interpretations.

Mrs. Beatrice Ryder answers your questions in non-technical language for all to understand. She is an experienced astrologer who has been consulted by many of the celebrated people in America and Europe because of her sympathetic and understanding revelations of the planetary influences on life. Her wisdom and humane attitude are most appealing. Birdfeather, leader of the under-thirty hippie star cult, magazine columnist and TV personality, has written a lively foreword. Her prediction is that your only problem with this book will be protecting it from the skeptics who will want to borrow it.

Petrus Apianus "Astronomicum Caesareum"

ASTROLOGY

Your Personal Sun-Sign Guide

by
Beatrice Ryder

Foreword by Birdfeather

1974 EDITION

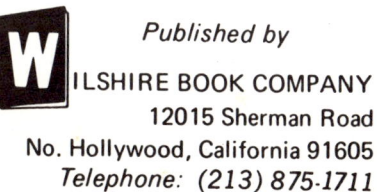

Published by
WILSHIRE BOOK COMPANY
12015 Sherman Road
No. Hollywood, California 91605
Telephone: (213) 875-1711

Frontispiece: Permission of The Metropolitan Museum of Art, Gift of Herbert N. Straus, 1925

Printed by
HAL LEIGHTON PRINTING CO.
P. O. Box 1231
Beverly Hills, California 90213
Telephone: (213) 346-8500

© Copyright, 1969 Fleet Press Corporation
156 Fifth Avenue
New York City 10010

All rights reserved

Library of Congress Catalogue Card No.: 77-90282

No portion of this book may be reprinted in any form without the **written** permission of the publisher, except by a reviewer who **wishes** to quote brief passages in connection with a review for a **newspaper,** magazine, or radio-television program.

Manufactured in the United States of America
ISBN 0-87980-006-2

FOREWORD

Beatrice Ryder, a native of the Sun-Sign Capricorn, writes with planetary awareness from over thirty years' experience as a practicing astrologer. Capricorns have always been known for their thoroughness in pursuing their chosen fields, and Mrs. Ryder is no exception.

Mrs. Ryder's interest in the occult dates from her early childhood when she demanded a telescope from her parents so that she could observe the stars and the motions of the planets. When she discovered that the planetary movements influence life on earth, she chose Astrology as a profession. She pursued her studies with the best teachers and by herself in the great libraries of Europe and America. While traveling in pursuit of knowledge she became acquainted with many prominent people in the social and theatrical worlds from whom she was to draw a large part of her clientele.

Realizing that others could benefit from her wide knowledge gained from reading and interpreting charts, Mrs. Ryder turned to writing to disseminate to a larger audience the practical advice for living which would help them cope better with the problems of today's complex way of life.

In reading this book I find that Mrs. Ryder's approach to Astrology is enlightening to the mind, yet simple enough to be understandable and helpful to all. In this it is most unique. Most books on Astrology are complex texts which require a knowledge of higher mathematics which can be most discouraging to the person who wishes to read and know, to benefit himself, and to enjoy the dawning of both knowledge and inspiration.

Whether you are a first-time reader of astrological lore or a learned scholar of the subject, you will find all the necessary information gathered in this volume: Sun-Sign and Decanate interpretations which let you see yourself (and others) in relationship to planetary orbits and motions; guidance for the evolution of your personal traits, glamor, career and marriage, and a definitive explanation of normal and abnormal love and sex.

Mrs. Ryder writes from both her mind and her heart. In this lies her true value as a friend and as a teacher.

Birdfeather

New York City
June, 1969

CONTENTS

I	How Astrology Works An explanation of your horoscope in simple terms	13
II	The Astrology Story A short history of the science of prediction based on planetary influences	18
III	The Ideal You How to fulfill your greatest innate potentials	31
IV	The Power of Your Personality Your inborn traits according to the Decan under which you were born	96
V	Stars and the Sex Syndrome Normal and abnormal sexuality in the horoscope	120
VI	The Star Keys to Power How each of the planets in your horoscope plays a part in giving you power traits	132
VII	Glamor in Your Horoscope How to channel your sex appeal and win what you want	145
VIII	Your Astrological Partner How to select your most compatible partner in business or marriage	159
IX	The Friendship Ring How to know people as they really are according to their horoscopes	169
X	The Magic in Colors The values of color related to planetary influences	184

XI	The Magic in Music	192
	How to attain harmony through the vibratory power of music selected according to your Sign	
XII	Your Psychic Self	200
	How to use the mystic powers of your super-faculties in everyday living	
XIII	Pets and Stars	215
	An explanation of the harmony between the animal and human kingdoms	

THE TWELVE SIGNS

OF THE

ZODIAC

Aries: March 21 to April 19

♈

Taurus: April 20 to May 20

♉

Gemini: May 21 to June 20

♊

Cancer: June 21 to July 22

♋

 Leo: July 23 to August 22

♌

 Virgo: August 23 to September 22

♍

 Libra: September 23 to October 23

 Scorpio: October 24 to November 22

♏

 Sagittarius: November 23 to December 21

 Capricorn: December 22 to January 19

 Aquarius: January 20 to February 18

 Pisces: February 19 to March 20

Chapter I

HOW ASTROLOGY WORKS

One of the oldest and most revered studies of mankind is Astrology. This is quite natural, for there is no spectacle in nature so awe-inspiring as that of the heavens with their ever changing wonders to behold. Since ancient times man has not ceased to wonder how the pageant of the stars has influenced his life.

In the olden days, before the building of cities, shepherds, as they tended their flocks, looked up to the celestial ceiling and felt the bond that tied the starry movements to their own. They observed that when the cluster of stars now known as the constellation Aries was in sight that it was the time of fertility, and associated it with the Ram. In this way, there grew up a tradition of "seasons" connected with the movement of the Sun (apparently) through the twelve Signs of the Zodiac.

As the study of the stars grew more complex, and instruments which permitted more accurate observation were invented, man's knowledge grew apace, so that now there are few secrets about the heavens that remain undiscovered.

The body of discovered knowledge is known as Astrology, the influence of the stars on life on this planet, Earth. The cosmic radiations emanating from the planets act as a stimulus on the tides, on vegetable and animal life, on the life beneath the surface of the seas, on the minerals beneath the surface of the earth, and on all that exists, grows, thrives, flourishes, subsists, endures, lives and breathes between heaven and earth!

If you had been able to take a picture of the heavens at the very moment of your birth, that photograph would be your horoscope. Since it is technically impossible to take such an actual photograph, a facsimile of the picture that would have been taken is made by an astrologer, and that facsimile is your horoscope. In other words, your horoscope is a representation of the skies with the planets placed in the correct positions they were in at the time you were born.

The skies as you see them overhead seem to form a circle. Actually, this view is elliptical but appears to be circular. Thus, we consider it to have the $360°$ which comprises a true circle. Now, visualize this circle divided into twelve equal parts. These twelve segments of $30°$ each are the twelve Signs of the Zodiac. As has been said, in the Spring a cluster of stars is visible in the first segment on the extreme left or easternmost point; this occurs when the Sun begins its round of the sky for the year. Because of the recurrence of this view, the first segment is named after the cluster of stars (or constellation) which appears in it, and is known as Aries. The other eleven segments or Signs are named after the constellations in them, as follows: the second, Taurus; the third, Gemini; the fourth, Cancer; the fifth, Leo; the sixth, Virgo; the seventh, Libra; the eighth, Scorpio; the ninth, Sagittarius; the tenth, Capricorn; the eleventh, Aquarius; the twelfth, Pisces.

There are two Luminaries in the Solar System: the Sun and the Moon. In addition to these two orbs, there are eight known planets: Mercury, Venus, Mars, Jupiter, Saturn, Uranus, Neptune and Pluto. For the sake of convenience, all these celestial bodies are referred to as planets, making ten in all.

As the ten planets are constantly moving in their orbits at phenomenal speed through the twelve Signs of the Zodiac, it is very easy to understand that a different pattern is formed from minute to minute. For this reason, every person has an individual horoscope, which is his and his alone.

The Sun is always in the first Sign of the Zodiac, Aries, from March 21st to April 21st (every year). Thus, people born between these dates are said to be born under the Sign of Aries. As the Sun apparently moves from one Sign to the next during the year, everyone is born under some Sign—called his Sun Sign—according to the date of his birth.

Since the other planets all move at varying rates of speed, they form different angles to each other from moment to moment. For example, if you were born when the Sun was in Aries and the Moon in Libra, these two Luminaries would be $180°$ apart, or opposite to each other. This aspect is therefore called an opposition.

Your destiny is therefore comprised of your Sun Sign, the position of each planet in a certain Sign, and the aspects the planets form to each other. These factors determine your character—and your character is the basis of your thoughts, actions, reactions, and therefore your fate.

In addition to the influence already mentioned, you have a ruling planet, for each Sign is governed by either a Luminary or a planet. Aries is ruled by Mars, Taurus by Venus, Gemini by Mercury, Cancer by the Moon, Leo by the Sun, Virgo by Mercury, Libra by Venus, Scorpio by Pluto, Sagittarius by Jupiter, Capricorn by Saturn, Aquarius by Uranus, and Pisces by Neptune.

As you look at the circular figure which is your chart or horoscope, you can count from the extreme left or easternmost point, known as the Ascendant, all around the twelve segments, going in a counter-clockwise direction. Counting in this manner tells you the Houses in your horoscope; thus the first 30 degree section is your First House; the second thirty degree section is your Second House; and so on. The reason that each segment is referred to as a "House" when it is the individual's chart that is being considered is that each segment governs a certain department of life, in the following order: the First governs personality; the Second, money; the Third, mentality; the Fourth, home; the Fifth, emotions; the Sixth, employment and health; the Seventh, marriage and partnership; the Eighth, desires; the Ninth, intuitions; the Tenth, career; the Eleventh, hopes; the Twelfth, faith.

Your birth chart never changes, of course, since it is a facsimile of planetary positions at the moment you began life. However, as the planets continuously move or transit, they take their places in new positions in the Houses of your horoscope, forming new aspects and influences as they do so. Your present life and your future life may be predicted by interpreting these positions, placements, and aspects because the astrologer can tell from his tables and books just where the planets are at any time.

The scholar of Astrology knows the meanings of these planetary motions from the wealth of the literature and research on the subject—which is the oldest study of mankind. Historical predictions made by astrologers have come true and have added to the store of knowledge available. The study and analysis of thousands of charts have shown that similar aspects have preceded similar events in people's lives. It may thus be seen that predictions can be correctly made, thanks to the research and patience that have been devoted to making Astrology a sound subject.

A NOTE ON YOUR SUN-SIGN

Because the calendar we use is man-made, it differs from "the clock in the sky which needs no winding." For this reason, the calendar always begins on January 1st. The sky calendar always starts on the 21st of March, the first day of Spring. Man's calendar must change during leap years to accommodate for the lunar basis for calculation.

Persons born on the cusp, the day before or after the transit of the Sun from one Sign to another, and who wish to check in which Sign the Sun was at the time of their birth may consult an ephemeris.

Chapter II

THE ASTROLOGY STORY

Whether it was Adam or Pithecanthropus erectus who was the first man, there can be no doubt that he looked up in wonder at the splendor and beauty of the stars!

Of course, we have the Scriptural record of the creation, and at the very beginning of Genesis is the lovely description of the "lights in the firmament of the heaven to divide the day from the night." Perhaps the very first mention of Astrology is given following this passage, in which God said, "and let them be for *signs,* and for seasons, and for days, and years."

For those of a scientific turn of mind, it must be mentioned that archeological ruins have yielded their treasures of the symbols of Astrology in cities buried under the sands of the deserts for countless centuries. Hoary manuscripts and ancient papyri have given their secrets to the Egyptologists and other scholars, and always the symbols of the star art appear as evidence of the knowledge of the subject as far back as we can probe.

As far back as astrological and historical research can delve in the river of time, it appears that one era of Astrology has merged into another, just as all forms of culture have done in the progress of civilization. Astrology can be traced back to its first recorded origins in the Tibetan and Hindu era, approximately existing from the year 5000 B.C. to 3000 B.C. As culture spread, the eras overlapped. In Egypt, Astrology dominated the years from 3000 B.C. to 1800 B. C. Chinese Astrology reigned from 2500 B.C. to 500 B.C. Then, also, the celestial science grew its deepest roots in Hebraic, Babylonian, and Chaldean culture between 2200 B.C. and 500 B.C.

The Greek era in Astrology existed for the thousand years between 1200 B.C. and 200 B.C. Then, in the early Christian Era, the Romans led the field. The tenth century A.D. is known as the age of Al-Biruni. In the dim days of the Crusades, little is recorded of the progress of the star art, until the Renaissance, when in the fourteenth and fifteenth centuries A.D., the palmy days came into their full rights.

THE IRON AGE

Mathematics is essential to the study of Astrology, as methodical calculations are necessary for understanding the motions of the heavenly bodies. The Hindus mastered this science of numbers, which is immortalized in their Tirvalore Tables of about the year 3000 B.C., which saw the opening of the Kali Yug, or Iron Age.

The Sun is represented by Vishnu in the Hindu scriptures or *Rigveda*. Vishnu is the life principle, thus the absolutely perfect astrological symbol, as there could be no physical animation on Earth were it not for the solar rays. According to Hindu philosophy, Vishnu passes through seven regions of the Earth (the mystic number), placing his footsteps in three directions; the latter are the Sun's rising place, the meridian, and the place of setting.

Vishnu is said to descend to Earth when human affairs are discordant; he comes in a superhuman form to set things right. The descent of the Hindu god in this manner is called an *avatara*, and the shapes he assumes are depicted on ancient temple walls, some dating back over seven thousand years. Some of these forms (avatara) are the Ram (Aries-fertility), the Bull (Taurus-strength), the Lion (Leo-victory), and other symbols, which may be the first recorded description of the symbols of the Zodiac.

Besides the Solar Zodiac, the Hindus divided the elliptic into twenty-eight equal parts, one for each of the star clusters or constellations whose boundaries were denoted by the diurnal progress of the Moon, and which were called lunar mansions.

The lunar years and other devices in Hindu Astrology show the more eastern trend, while the Solar Zodiac became the principal foundation or basis of the Astrology in Greece and Egypt. Thus the western world's inhabitants have become known as the "children of the Sun," and the Eastern world's as the "children of the Moon."

In the classic Hindu *Bala Kanda* the horoscope of the god

Rama is given. From the data therein, of astronomical character, it is deducible that it is the chart for a person born before the year 3100 B.C., perhaps one of the first pieces of historical evidence of Hindu Astrology's antiquity.

The distinguished Indian scholar Sastri considers the Hindus the oldest surviving people in the world, and Astrology their oldest art. India, which was the cradle of the system of numbers or numerals now known to the world, thus seems also to have fostered the first study of the stars.

EGYPTIAN KNOWLEDGE

At the Egyptian Museum at Turin, there is a papyrus of the Twentieth Dynasty on which extremely ancient horoscopes are preserved, showing the antiquity of Astrology in Egypt. A manuscript of the third century B.C. was discovered by M. W. Dundel. It is entitled *Liber Hermetis,* and its contents display a remarkable independence of Egyptian Astrology from Chaldean Astrology. It is established that the Egyptians attribute their knowledge of the celestial art to the god Thot, who instructed them. But, the teachings were aimed at spiritual enlightenment (as was Hindu Astrology), and it was not until much later that the star knowledge was applied to material human affairs.

Still, the knowledge of star positions and movements, which was kept secret or esoteric by the authorities and priests, enabled them to build the monuments that remain standing today as eternal symbols of their genius. We today can but grope for the meanings in our heritage. Thus, we can see in the Great Sphinx, half-human, and half-bestial, a symbol of Sagittarius, one of the most beautiful of the constellations.

And we know that the pyramids, whose architecture is still a mystery even to modern science, were so built as to point to and reveal certain stars or planets, known to the ancient royal architects. But on the whole, the prophecy of Hermes Trismegistus has been fulfilled: "O Egypt, Egypt! Nothing will remain of your great thought and mysteries for future generations but some signs cut into stone and indecipherable to common mortals. But they will suffice to immortalize you in the centuries of centuries."

Chinese classical literature is filled with references to the "divine science," because *to divine* is *to predict*. The origin of Astrology in China is ascribed to the Divine Emperor, Fu Hsi, who is believed to have lived and reigned about 2800 B.C., and to have been a student of the occult and revealed to man his knowledge of divination of the planets.

As the Chinese had no knowledge of an outside world, and this latter world was ignorant of the very existence of China, it is easy to understand that Chinese Astrology originated within its own borders. An ancient Chinese document known as the "Great Plan" contains the principles of Chinese Astrology, and correlates moral conduct with the motion of the Sun, Moon, and planets, establishing the Yin and Yang, or negative and positive concepts. The latter idea, over four thousand years old, it should be noted, is no different from today's idea of negative and positive forces in the atomic theory!

Before the year 2000 B.C., it was reported in the annals of the Emperor Yao that His Imperial Highness divided the twelve Signs of the Zodiac by the twenty-eight mansions of the Moon, giving evidence of the brilliance and antiquity of Chinese Astrology.

THE CHALDEAN INFLUENCE

The first of all the esoteric sciences of the Chaldeans which was to bring them renown throughout the known world was the study of the stars.

The philosopher, Philon, wrote: "The Chaldeans were the first to think that the good and evil of every individual depends on the Sun and the planets." Diodorus of Sicily wrote: "Having observed the stars for an enormous number of years, the Chaldeans knew more exactly than all other men their course and their influence, and predicted exactly the things of the future."

Another great authority, Lenormant, said that the known world in the days of the Chaldeans recognized the latter as their incontestable masters in this branch of divination. Chaldean Astrology was the first astronomy in the culture of the world, which the Greeks adopted, and to which the modern world has fallen heir.

The famous tower of Babel was built to learn the secrets of the heavens. In imitation thereof, the Chaldeans built the ziggurat, a type of pyramid, of which Herodotus has left an accurate description. "Each step was six meters high, and there were seven steps; the first was painted white, the second black, the third red, the fourth blue, the fifth vermillion, the sixth gray, and the seventh gold, the color of the Sun. On the summit was an observatory... called a khorsabad."

In the ziggurat at Nineveh were found by modern researchers the astrological tables and documents which reveal that the Chaldeans distinguished the planets, the stars, the Moon, and the Sun. Diodorus ascribes the invention of the Zodiac to the Chaldeans, for they divided the Sun's visits to the twelve Houses (Signs), each of which was divided into three equal parts (Decans), and each governed by a "counselor" (planetary ruler).

The Sun, the Moon, and the five (then) known planets were placed into three categories:

1. Jupiter and Venus, two beneficent stars, which were called (even then) the greater and lesser Fortune.

2. Saturn and Mars, the two infortunes, also called the greater and lesser Infortune.

3. The Sun, the Moon, and Mercury, of propitious or unfortunate influence according to their position or aspect.

Each day was considered under the rulership of the planet which governed the Sign that was rising at one minute after midnight.

The Chaldeans had precise rules for the effect of every phase of the Moon, and they predicted accurately national events of a mundane nature, as well as the weather, from these carefully worked out points.

The horoscopes worked out for the kings were accurate prophecies, all of which eventually came to pass, cases in point being Darius, Alexander the Great, Emperor Antigone, and King Saleucus Nicanos. When the records were discovered, the scholars were truly struck with admiration for the "divine science."

There are many references to the stars and star lore in the Old Testament, bearing testimony to the Jews' knowledge of Astrology. In Job, one finds a reference to the influence of the stars: "Canst thou bind the sweet influences of the Pleiades, or loose the bands of Orion?" In Judges, there is another such reference: "The stars in their courses fought against Sisera." Of the will of the stars, one finds this note in Job: "Canst thou guide Arcturus with his sons?"

Pythagoras, the Greek philosopher, was thought to be the first to speak of the "music of the spheres," yet in the Book of Job one learns that the Hebrews were already familiar with this: "The morning stars sang together, and all the sons of God shouted for joy."

In the sixth century B.C., the prophet Ezekiel did much to spread the popularity of the Book of Job throughout the land of Macedonia.

Abraham, the Chaldean prophet, was honored by kings and populace for his predictions, which were said to have been made possible through the use of an astrological tablet which he wore for the purposes of divination and prophecy.

Both Josephus and Ibn Ezra, two of the greatest of recorders of the history of the Jews, accredit these people with special wisdom and knowledge of the heavenly bodies, and they trace the history of the Zodiac as far back as Seth, son of Adam. However, these scholars give what would be called only circumstantial evidence for their theory of this antiquity of the Zodiac's history.

GREEK ASTROLOGY

That the Greeks had a vital influence on Astrology is attested by the fact that the word Zodiac stems from *zodion,* the diminutive of the Greek word *zoon,* which means animal, and which stands for the beasts' outlines as conceived in the star cluster outlines which are called constellations.

Nectanebus, the Egyptian magician and astrologer, went to Greece, where he attended Olympias, and advised her on the propitious moment to bear her son, who was to become Alexander the Great, a moment calculated according to the position of the heavenly bodies, and said to have been heralded by a pageant of splendor in the skies.

It was during Alexander's reign that numerous Chaldean astrologers went to dwell in Athens, Berosus, who had been a priest of Belus at Babylonia and had written a history of Chaldea (preserved in part by Eusebius), translated the *Treatise on Astrology,* of Sargon I and founded a school of astronomy at Cos.

Berosus taught the art of reading destiny in the stars, and his success was such that the Athenians erected a statue to him in the Gymnasium. The statue of Berosus was represented as holding a golden lyre in its hand, the symbol of the accuracy of his predictions.

Other Chaldean astrologers became celebrated in Athens, and were greatly honored. Among these were Astrampsychos, Gabrya, and Pazatas. Many of these celebrities among the magicians and astrologers were immortalized in the *Characters* by the writer Theophrastus.

The father of Euripides, great classical Greek playwright, had a horoscope cast on the birth of his son which predicted, and accurately, a rare celebrity and fame.

It was a Greek astrologer, Hipparchus, who discovered the procession of the equinoxes, one of the stepping-stones to knowledge of the stars.

The most celebrated Greek astrologer was Aratus, born at Soli in the third century B.C., and equally famed as an astronomer and poet. He visited the court of Ptolemy, and was then called to Macedonia by Antigone Gonathas, who held him in high esteem. His poem, *Phenomena,* is a full discourse on the astrological philosophy of his times.

The Ptolemaic astrological system was the first to correlate color and metal rulership to the planets. According to their system, the following rulerships were ascribed:

Planet	Color	Metal
Sun	gold	gold
Moon	silver	silver
Saturn	gray	lead
Jupiter	white	electrum
Mars	red	zinc
Venus	yellow	copper
Mercury	variable	quicksilver

Plato, first of the world's great thinkers and philosophers, employed Astrology as a key to the order of the universe. He called the stars divine, eternal, ever-abiding, and in his *Republic,* he describes the music of the spheres, the seven planets, and the eighth sphere of the fixed stars. He refers to the spindle of necessity—reincarnation—and was the first to reveal the theory of cycles!

THE ROMAN DEVOTEES

The Romans were sincere devotees of Astrology. Among the famous Romans who believed in the star art were Mark Antony, Augustus Caesar, Tiberius, and Nero. They both consulted astrologers, and practiced themselves.

In Shakespeare's *Julius Caesar,* which everyone has studied, the most remembered line is the warning of the soothsayer to Caesar, "Beware the Ides of March." This famous incident is based on the actual meeting between Caesar and an astrologer named Vestritus Spurinna. History soon bore out the truth of the astrologer's prediction.

The Romans used tables or calendars of good and adverse days which were based on planetary aspects, and calculated by astrologers. The latter were officially appointed "augurs" who professionally advised and counseled the priests and rulers through their divining arts.

Cicero himself wished to become an augur, for the position held renown, respect, and rewards. Despite his concentration and study, he could not make the grade. The spark to divine just was not there, and so he became very spiteful on the subject of Astrology, but his bitter philippics were renounced by the great poets Horace, Ovid, and Juvenal whose immortal classics are replete with praiseworthy allusions to the mysterious art of the stars.

Apollonius of Tyana, fragments of whose astrological treatises still are preserved, was held in awe by the Roman emperors, and venerated simultaneously for his knowledge and power. Hadrian kept a journal in which he noted his astrological predictions, all of which were fulfilled, including that of his own demise.

The most celebrated works on Astrology in Roman times were the encyclopedias of Nechepso and of Petorisis. These were considered the classics of the times, and were used for daily consultation by the most noted Roman citizens from the time of Sylla to that of Tiberius.

As Rome declined from world leadership and eminence, so did Astrology recede in popularity there. The interest of the public waned, but the scholars privately continued their studies and research. In all ages there have been elected souls whose function was to preserve occult knowledge and to pass it on to the next generation. Then when the appointed time arrives, the vessel of this secret knowledge once more enlightens the populace. For a period of time following the fall of Rome, Astrology and the occult sciences might be said to have gone underground.

While western Astrology may thus be said to have been on the wane, eastern Astrology was waxing in stature and progress. The astrological historical period which followed the Roman era was called the Age of Al-Biruni, so named after the author of the *Tafhim*. His age was the eleventh century, which was the blossoming time of Mohammedan culture and the climax of medieval thought.

The *Tafhim* is a tome of instruction on the principles of Astrology and the related sciences, geometry, astronomy, geography, and chronology. Al-Biruni wrote: "I have begun with geometry, proceeded to arithmetic, and the science of numbers, then to the structure of the universe, and finally to judicial Astrology, for no one is worthy of the style and title of astrologer who is not conversant with these four sciences."

In the times from Dante to Shakespeare, Astrology, like the phoenix, rose again. The Palmy Days, as they were called by historians, were but the precursors of modern Astrology, the discovery of "new" planets, and the application of scientific research principles to the oldest and most noble of the branches of knowledge known to man.

The names of Dr. Dee, William Lilly, and Nostradamus fill the pages of history with their almost blinding brilliance. The uncanny prescience of these scholars brought Astrology back into the great repute and popularity which it enjoys today.

The New International Encyclopedia closes its excellent section on Astrology with the following words:

"Predictions of the better class of astrologers are not mere haphazard guesses, as is frequently supposed, but are based upon rightly scientific determination from observed phenomena, according to definite rules of interpretation." The history of human culture is a parallel to the history of man's interest in, and growing knowledge of, the stars.

Chapter III

THE IDEAL YOU

INTRODUCTION

Your individuality is indestructible. When you were born, the horoscope for your nativity endowed you with ideal traits of character. The changes in your personality occur because of the transits and aspects formed through the years in your chart. By knowing the perfection with which you are innately endowed, you can strive to regain it. Each of these Sign portraits will inspire you with the depiction of your true self. Each will also reveal the true picture of anyone you know according to his or her Sign.

ARIES: March 21 to April 19

In the springtime of the year, the Earth is reborn. The spiritual rejuvenation that takes place on the planet you inhabit is symbolic of the Sign under which you were born—Aries—the beginning of the zodiacal year. You can enjoy the same spiritual reincarnation, too.

As the planets progress through the Signs of the Zodiac, a myriad of changes takes place in nature and in man. However, the basic *you* never changes. Your natal chart always remains the same. It is the mirror of the celestial pattern at the time of your birth.

For this reason, you can live up to the ideals and aspirations with which you were endowed at birth. You can fulfill the pattern of the Ideal You as represented in your horoscope. Therefore, you should make the effort to *become* the Ideal You.

Your potentialities are presented in the word image of the Ideal You given herewith. Visualize yourself as the person in the image. Live up to the ideals, standards, and qualifications of this Sun-Sign delineation, for it is your best self. Reflect the person in this portrait by acting as he would. Ask for help and guidance to develop into this ideality in your prayers and meditations. Think and act like the Ideal You in order to become it.

Mars is the governing planet of the Sign under which you were born, and endows you with many qualities which, although they have a "martial" touch, are not at all setbacks. Indeed, they give the positive touch to what might otherwise be pale or weak facets in your nature.

You have vision. You see yourself at the helm of a ship discovering new lands and opening up new vistas to others. The spunk and spirit of the pioneers is in you, and you go forth to break the trail at the head of the group which looks to you for leadership.

No hardship can take you from the path or turn your feet backward. You do not know what it means to give up but in your earnest and determined manner go on, forging ahead, pushing obstacles aside, and finally getting to the goal which you set out to reach.

Your energy is boundless, your courage omnipotent. Fear is unknown to you, and opposition you do not even recognize.

These are the qualities by which the world knows you, but you have an inner life, too, that you do not share except with people whom you have found truly congenial. The life of the mind is just as active (perhaps more so) as the very busy career you have on the material plane. You are a scholar, and poring over new and old books, discovering a gem here and a pearl of wisdom there, gives you great pleasure. You love wit, whether you find it in a book or in a conversation. In your own group, you like to tell a story and act it out. For the exercise of your charm and brilliance you like an audience of the same mental caliber as yourself. Your mind is ever active, and you are therefore never at a loss for entertainment, whether you are alone or in a crowd.

The domineering aspect of your nature reveals itself only when your aim is for the greatest good for the greatest number. Otherwise you do not force issues, because you are sensitive to the requirements of all people as individuals with their own ideas and rights. Your ideas are progressive, and your pleasing and magnetic personality draws to you many people who follow you because they see the nobility and generosity that you represent.

Paradoxical as it may seem for a leader and very independent person, you crave warmth and affection for yourself, and you are ardent and romantic. However, it is not a case of "the world well lost" when you are in love; it is a case of your going out to conquer the world so that you may lay it at the feet of your beloved as a gift.

You like order and harmony. It may seem at times that your love of order takes picayune forms, for you do get upset when your things are disturbed; but the symbol is an important one. You like the same order, regularity, and peace to exist all around you; you seek to establish it, and that is mighty important in the world today. Your personal tastes extend even a little further, for you have a great admiration for the luxurious, and a deep-set appreciation of the sensual.

A Classic Example of Aries

Thomas Jefferson was born under the Sign Aries on April 13, 1743. He represents the finest qualities of the typical Aries-born individual. No other individual in the history of our nation has had such a profound influence.

To say that Jefferson had the vision typical of the Aries-born is to give an example that should be classical. It was he who framed and wrote the Declaration of Independence, most noble document in the history of liberal thought.

Jefferson was born at Shadwell, Virginia. He practiced law and farming before he went into public life, and always retained a deepseated love for his native state. Seeking always the improvement of his fellow man, he founded the University of Virginia. His generous and progressive character was soon recognized by the electorate, and at twenty-six years of age, he was sent to the House of Burgesses.

So fertile was his mind that advancement after advancement came to him in rapid succession. In turn he was a member of the Continental Congress, Governor of Virginia, Representative to France, member of Washington's Cabinet, Vice-President, and President for two terms.

Like all those born under Aries, his abounding energy could not be restricted to one career or one outlet. He was a prolific writer, and the best one of his time. But he was equally the greatest architect of his time. His commercial treaties were as great as his political documents.

The martial progress of the Aries-born Jefferson never halted. At seventy-three, full of hope and optimism, he wrote to former President John Adams, who had been his friend for fifty years, that he certainly would like to live his whole life all over again. He reveals the mental keenness, understanding, and sympathy of the Aries-born in this letter, as well as the courage and fearlessness of the Mars-ruled: "I think that it is a good world on the whole; that it has been framed on a principle of benevolence, and more pleasure than pain dealt out to us. There are indeed (who might say nay?), gloomy and hypochondriac minds, inhabitants of diseased bodies, disgusted with the present and despairing of the future; always counting that the worst will happen, because it may happen. To these I say, how much pain have cost us the evils which have never happened! My temperament is sanguine. I steer my bark with Hope in the head, leaving Fear astern."

Let these concluding words be your slogan. Take this image of the Ideal You and this noble example of a man as your inspiration. Be sanguine; have hope; abandon fear. By taking your innate courage into your hands and living the Ideal You, you will become the Ideal You.

TAURUS: April 20 to May 20

*The fault, dear Brutus, is not in our stars,
But in ourselves, that we are underlings.*

Through the multitude of references to Astrology in Shakespeare's works, we know he had a vast understanding of the subject. In the quotation above, from *Julius Caesar,* we again appreciate his understanding of human nature from his knowledge of Astrology.

These words do not apply only to Brutus to whom they were addressed; they apply to you! When you were born, the stars—that is to say, the planets, the luminaries, and the constellations—formed a pattern in the skies directly above the place of your birth. Fleeting though this design might have been because of the astronomical speed with which the heavenly bodies move, it formed your horoscope, which any efficient astrologer can reproduce with accuracy.

There are no "faults in your stars" or in your horoscope. All the potentialities with which you were endowed are to be read therein. And, because your birthchart never changes, those forces and powers are still alive in you. Those traits comprise the Ideal You. For this reason, even though time and circumstances have changed you to outward appearances, or in your thoughts and habits, you can still express the best of your star-heritage.

You are herewith presented a picture of the Ideal You, based upon the position of the Sun at the time of your birth, and the influence of the planetary governor of your Sign.

You are indubitably the most selfless person in your own group, for your thoughts and impulses are all aimed toward helping others. Your kindness and magnanimity know no bounds, and your generosity is such that you give to others freely of yourself.

You have much money sense in the limited, material meaning of the word, and you have a real sense of its great value to do good. It may seem to you that you will never end the calculating to make ends meet, but a moment's reflection will demonstrate that you are really parting with money for the joy it gives you to be kind, thoughtful, generous, and helpful to others.

Entertaining is one of your chief pleasures. In your home, not only do you like to give others a good time, but you have one yourself. Like everything else you do, your entertainment provides the best of surroundings and refreshments. You know how to mix people, and even in a crowd you know just how to make each person feel that he or she is getting your individual attention. These social graces make your home a popular gathering place, and you are looked up to as the leader and organizer of your group.

Great zeal distinguishes your intellectual pursuits. When you set out to learn anything—from driving a car to mastering a foreign language—you do so with such enthusiasm and determination that you learn with amazing rapidity. A fearless quality holds you to your course, and obstacles that would discourage the average person are only stimulating challenges to you.

With your powers of organization, you rise rapidly to the top of any group with which you become affiliated. Your spirited energy is soon recognized, as is your magnetic power which draws additional members, protagonists, or adherents. Because you are efficient and penetrating, you cut red-tape to the minimum and get things done.

A Classic Example of Taurus

The greatest of all naturalists, John James Audubon, was born under Taurus, on April 26, 1785, at Santo Domingo. This author and painter of *Birds of North America* was educated in America and France, and settled on his father's farm near Philadelphia in 1804.

Under the cruel laws of the nineteenth century he was even imprisoned for debt, but his faithful wife came to his rescue. Through all his reverses and suffering, he never lost sight of his aim: to devote his life to the high purpose of preserving forever in the gorgeous hues from his palette, the birds of the North American continent in their natural habitat.

Despite an undisciplined youth provided by an indulgent father, he displayed the zeal and determination of those born under Taurus in learning how to paint—a vocation directed by the rulership of Venus over his Sign.

He became photographically proficient in his painting of birds, and finally achieved fame. Toward the end of his career this fame became almost a myth. Venus colors the creative imagination, however, and although his paintings were faithful reproductions of the creatures of nature, the anecdotes that accompanied them were tinted with sentimental tones. Taurus loves the best and the most dramatic. In his youth Audubon was a great dandy, apparelled always in the latest fashions. Because his search for his bird models took him to their habitats, remote from civilized centers, he adopted the costume of the frontiersman. He alternated between his labors in nature's haunts and his lavish entertainments at the mansion he built on Riverside Drive in New York. He was the hardest of workers when he worked, and the hardest of players when he played.

Of the work of Audubon, it can be said that no one left a greater monument to his own determination nor a greater legacy to his adopted land. He painted nearly two thousand life-sized figures of birds, almost five hundred of them in full color, set in their natural environment. What patience, what invention, what discomfort went into this life work can be known only to a naturalist who has tried to observe nature unobserved.

In 1937 a centenary edition of the colored plates was issued, thus making available to almost everyone what had long been one of the most expensive and prized books in any collector's library.

Audubon never lost sight of his aim. Hardship and obstacles could not deter him. There is the strength of Taurus, the ability to win through in the end.

You can fulfill the potentialities of the Ideal You. Never despair; always bear in mind the destiny of mankind—to achieve—because all men are gods in the becoming. On the wheel of life, make this incarnation a realization of the Ideal You.

GEMINI: May 21 to June 20

Look back into your life to the time when you were fifteen years old. You had then completed two seven year cycles, and were at a turning point. Behind you were childhood and elementary schooling. Before you were hopes, dreams, aspirations, and a picture you had of your future—the Ideal You.

What has become of that picture? Changing home conditions, the economic struggle and emotional upsets have made a vast difference between that picture of yourself and what you are today.

Yet, the light of Astrology on the conduct of your life might have led you directly to that goal which you cherished as a child upon the brink of life. You have not developed into the Ideal You because you have lost that picture.

Visualization is one of the best known, but perhaps least used, of occult principles. If you had kept the picture of the Ideal You before you steadily, you might by now have become the living image of it. Uncertainty, tension, worry, and fear have dimmed the image that Astrology could have made more vivid.

It is not too late to become the Ideal You.

But it takes thought and action.

You can begin now by using the principle of visualization. Construct a mental image of yourself, using the traits and qualities with which the planets have endowed you because of your birth under the Sign Gemini.

Traditionally, Gemini being a double-sign, duality is the clue to your nature. You are a person of both thought and action. Action sustains life, and is simultaneously the product of life. Your thought leads to knowledge, and knowledge leads to conduct or behavior. It is not the repetition of hosannahs which brings you nearer to the Ideal You, but action.

You measure your innate qualities by their outward forms. Your thoughts, concepts, theories, and ideals can be measured largely by your conduct, the externality of their expression. The ceaselessly changing order of the planets is an act of God. The creation of man in His image is an act. Being created in His image gives us all creative imagination. We must put this vivid but quiescent force to work to win the highest reward of possessing it. A single act exceeds a thousand incantations.

Mercury is your Sun dispositor, and is the donor of the silver tongue. In making an impression on other people, you express yourself most emphatically through speech. The Mercury influence on your ideal self enhances all the vocal arts—spoken voice and singing, the dramatic arts and opera, screen, television, and radio, as the mode of self-expression.

The seeds of greatness are within you. The duality of your nature can be made a great asset because the two natures are extremely opposite. Thus, it follows, makes the higher nature very, very high.

Your thirst for knowledge, endowed by the planetary ruler of the mind, Mercury, keeps you ever alert to the intellectual advancement in your environment. You cover a wide range in your reading, but books about the arts and sciences particularly appeal to you. You are impatient with anything not in good taste, and therefore may be a real critic.

To those you love, your generosity is great. You do not let the outlay perturb you, for you have high respect for the significance of the act of giving.

Tolerance is your personal watchword. This does not make you a rabid crusader in the cause of tolerance; you are not so extreme as to hit the next fellow on the head to convert him to your cause. But in a rational and therefore much more effective way you champion democratic principles and freedoms. By precept and your own example, you can be a better bit of propaganda for tolerance than a whole printed campaign.

Your Sun disposition makes you by nature mercurial. Variety is verily the spice of life to you. Travel and change are your dreams or relaxation. Port-au-Prince, Bengali, Madras—the tangy names of romantic ports-of-call stir the depths of your being, and you can respond to the music they stir in you.

A Classic Example of Gemini

Nature has a particular appeal to Gemini. Nor are your reactions merely to her outward forms. The soul of the visible creations of the mother earth is bared to you. It was no "accident" that Ralph Waldo Emerson, first and greatest American transcendentalist, was born under Gemini. Although he never renounced his belief in the Creator of all this beauty, he was impelled to give up his pulpit because he felt that orthodox, organized religion was too limited. He thought and expressed himself in universal terms. He was the first and foremost scholar and proponent of oriental thought in America. Yet his influence upon our ways of thought and living—the American way—remains indelible.

As a native of Gemini, Emerson is the outstanding example of the idealist who lived his ideals. He made the sacrifices necessary to becoming his ideal self with full confidence that his material needs would be more than filled by his living up to his noblest urges. As poet, philosopher, and lecturer, he was that strange anomaly—a wise man revered as a prophet in his own land as well as in all the nations of the world.

The profound understanding of nature which Emerson had is part of the Ideal You. You fully comprehend that man is ministered to materially by nature and that he is both part of the process and the result.

Beauty is the mark God sets upon virtue. The Ideal You is well-formed, clear-eyed, and upright. Age cannot wither the youth of your outlook nor the eternal hope in your heart.

Your greatest aspiration is to live the higher life. The tinkling temptations of a tawdry way of life hold no attractions for the Ideal You. The life of reason is the inspiration of your conduct. The spiritual glow of your inner life comes from the intuitive knowledge that immortality is your laurel wreath.

This is the astrological portrait of the Ideal You. Visualize it in order to attain it. Form it as a clear mental picture of yourself. Determine that this is the attainment you really desire. Open every portal of receptivity to it. Act upon every high aspiration every day. Live up to your highest and noblest impulses, and you will become the very image of the Ideal You.

CANCER: June 21 to July 22

In June, millions of children are graduated from schools all over the country. Think back to the day of receiving your diploma. It marked the end of one period in your life, and the beginning of another.

Didn't you go somewhere alone with that diploma and make a high resolve? You saw your future spread before you in a shining panorama—college—success—marriage—children—happiness—prestige. The picture you formed of yourself was the Ideal You.

Now look into the mirror, and into the reflection of your soul. What has become of the Ideal You? That picture has been dimmed by the conflict of modern times, tension caused by the pace of living, vague fears and apprehensions of an uncertain future.

Astrology might have preserved the mental picture of the Ideal You, and you might by now have been the living image of that picture. The most ancient of sciences, Astrology, can paint the portrait of the Ideal You from your ruling planets which endow you with specific traits. Your chart can plot the course of the future.

It is never too late to improve, but it requires concentration on your part. Your stars form a brilliant pattern for you, but it is up to you to breathe life into it. The delineation provided for you here can help you regain what you have lost; it is the Ideal You born under the Water Sign Cancer. Concentrate on this picture: make a mental image in which you are re-endowed with every facet, trait, and quality that is your star-heritage. Hold this in your mind constantly, that you may grow into it.

Patience brings all things; it is the very "Open Sesame" to Paradise for the Cancer born. You may thereby achieve every worthy hope, wish, and desire of your innermost ego, for patience stands above every other trait you have. Who has not heard how Griselde and Penelope were rewarded for their patience? Who has not learned from them that all things come to him who waits, as they will to you? You can accomplish enduring works with your patience; your power and strength can be developed with it. Like the alchemist's stone, this virtue transmutes human beings into spiritual beings.

You can hold fast to what you have, for having been born under the rulership of the Moon, you are endowed with determination and tenacity. Aspirations and loyalties remain forever yours, for like Hamlet to his friends, you "grapple them to your soul with bands of steel." This attitude is particularly to be noted in your relationship with those whom you hold dear. From devotion to your country down to a tender love for your immediate family, you have the sympathetic sensitivity that is often synonymous with adoration. This is no mere sloppy sentimentalism with you; you can fight to the finish to defend a cause or person whose rights you consider are being attacked.

In the passage of time, learning and experience cause culture to flower in you. Rare gifts are disclosed as the petals unfold, and your perception and understanding seem universal. Your intuition appears to be boundless, and as your ruler, the Moon, looks down upon the night vagaries of the world's waifs, you too can comprehend all things without condemning.

Your conscientious heart, however, desires progress for humanity. You want to see the world a better place, and you feel that in your charge a program of amelioration could not fail. The public good is your concern, and waste, poverty, mismanagement, crime, and inefficiency distress you. You penetrate purposefully into the breast of humanity, and with no bluenose or black umbrella, could happily cut out the tumors of society.

Leadership is your forte. The Moon reigns over the domain of personality, so you do not have the unfortunate trait of possessing constructive impulses without the creative talent to execute them. You are brave and courageous in introducing your platform for the way things should be done, and you calmly set about carrying it out. In this program you seek to establish the beautiful and the artistic as the standards for your environment because you hate ugliness as much as you do dishonesty.

The tenacity which colors your conduct also tints your remembrance of things past. Luna is the ruler of memory and makes you cling to all associations and objects of days gone by. Science, ever seeking to crumble obsolete theories of time and space, could set you up as an example of the merging of all seasons into the now. Memories, souvenirs, curios, the acquisitions, material and spiritual, of a lifetime, are ever yours to conjure up for nostalgia's sake.

Sensitive to a high degree, you take the poetic view of things and see them in a romantic light. For this reason, vulgarity is distasteful to you, as it is to most of your Sign who, as a poet once said, "taste the gentle Moon." This makes you mild in manner when in repose as well as fierce when aroused. Your kindness and politeness win you gentle and intellectual friends with whom you share the pleasures of the mind.

The Moon rules the masses. You, in some capacity, are before the public. Often with prophetic vision you seek to direct the destiny of the populace or to play your role in that web with high integrity. For this reason the theater and education attract you, as does social service. In time of stress, the seas, whose tides are the concern of your ruling luminary, attract you to the defense of their freedom. In perfectly deliberate conduct along these as well as social lines, you act on psychic impressions which you experience, for experience has taught you that your "hunch" is as good as the next fellow's plodding deductions.

A Classic Example of Cancer

Your optimistic perseverence is the ultimate ability of a human to vanquish despair and oppression. Miss Helen Keller, born June 27, 1880, under the Sign of Cancer, was stricken in childhood with an illness that left her blind, mute, and deaf. Yet, despite these handicaps, she lived to become one of the most prominent women of our times.

Miss Keller was noted for her re-learning to speak and to master several languages, to receive the written and spoken communications of others through her fingertips, and for her autobiography and numerous other inspired writings. Outstanding, however, was her typically Cancerian work in the field of social service for the benefit of the blind all over the world. With will-power and courage she established an endowed institution for the care of those afflicted as she was. With driving determination she persuaded state legislatures to set up boards for the care and rehabilitation of the sightless.

The self-sacrificing nature of Miss Keller's work is characteristic of the Moon-ruled. Yet this gracious and compassionate lady retained a twinkling sense of humor through every tribulation. What more selfless summing-up have we than her own words: "Silence sits immense upon my soul. Then comes hope with a smile and whispers, 'There is joy in self-forgetfulness.' So I try to make the light in others' eyes my Sun, the music in others' ears my symphony, the smile on others' lips my happiness."

You can overcome all obstacles. Perfect your work, and you perfect yourself. This product, the perfected ego, is the Ideal You.

Keep this picture before you constantly, allowing it to guide your every act. By being constructive and creative in your thoughts and deeds, you will eliminate the negative and print the positive of this photograph of the Ideal You.

LEO: July 23 to August 22

A great philosopher once expressed the thought that in the heart of every grown-up there is a child. That child, which you once were, retains the aspirations, hopes and ideals of the untroubled domain of youth. It is the Ideal You.

What has become of it? The external self and the mind have changed with experience. Family life and its responsibilities, rivalry for social recognition, competition in the economic world, the stress of modern existence, and the tempo of a world geared for war have paled the picture of your true self.

However, you may employ the occult principle of visualization to become more perfect. The deteriorating changes wrought by time can be erased by the analytical phase of Astrology, which functions to paint the portrait of your possibilities from the traits endowed upon you of Leo by your governing ruler, the Sun. You are born under the middle Sign of the Fire triplicity, and a vivid imagination may therefore be put to good use to help you unfold, once you know what you can be.

Absorb the word picture provided here, and hold it clearly in your mind. At all times, see yourself as you are depicted here. Feel yourself "growing into" this portrait, and conduct yourself strictly according to its standards. Open your receptivity to the prestige due to the person in this cameo, and you will evolve into that being.

Bear in mind that word, "conduct." You must *act* in order to become. Visualize; idealize; *act!* Live the Ideal You!

The most potent forces in the universe are yours to command. Entrusted in your control are the greatest powers, for the Sun—source of the life principle—is the ruler of your Sign. Lofty thoughts, beauty of nature and the cultural heritage of the race are your cosmic birthright.

You possess a fine musical appreciation, and rhythm characterizes all you do. The arts and literature elevate you to the heights of the pleasures of the mind. Your inner voice, the expression of discriminating taste, always tells you what is good, what is not.

A very sympathetic nature makes you understanding and helpful. The comfort of others is of prime concern in your thoughts. This does not mean that you leap into situations, for an innate delicacy prevents you from pushing yourself where you are not sure you're wanted. However, once you give your friendship, you are a friend for life. Charm goes hand in hand with generosity, and you need never lack a wide circle of admirers.

You have a philosophical outlook on life which stands you in good stead. The vicissitudes which wreck others, you take in your stride, because you have excellent insight. Your perspicacity and intuition are highly developed—a process that seems to take place within you unconsciously. Knowledge, skills, and information come to your assistance from hidden depths within you when the occasion demands.

Courage is your coat-of-arms. You never retire from the field of contest when the joust is for the right. Neither do you toady or seek advancement through favor. Full confidence in your own abilities to attain your inherent high aspirations carries you forward.

A Classic Example of Leo

Like your ruler, the Sun, you seek to enlighten the world It is therefore understandable that the greatest "messenger of light" in modern times was born under Leo—Helena Petrovna Blavatsky, "H. P. B." The author of *Isis Unveiled* and *The*

Secret Doctrine achieved universal fame for her work in spiritually illuminating hundreds of thousands of followers.

H. P. B. devoted her life to spreading a gospel of truth and to doing beneficent work for humanity. In the face of seemingly insurmountable obstacles—illness, ignorance, and enmity—she used her power of will to educate a reluctant public. She was indubitably the world's greatest occultist of modern times.

The profundity of the wisdom of this teacher and the depth of her desire to impart her knowledge are expressed in these words from *The Voice of the Silence,* "Learn to discern the real from the false, the ever-fleeting from the everlasting. Learn above all to separate head-learning from soul-wisdom, the 'Eye' from the 'Heart' doctrine."

The discernment and separation mentioned in this quotation comprise the discrimination which characterizes the Leo-born. Your standards are high, and you are sincerely devoted to them. Your association with people is on the conventional plane, but your thoughts soar to such heights as to transcend crystallized custom.

The emotions are high-lighted in your make-up. The sympathy you have for people in general is a tender affection for your acquaintances and a deep love for your true friends and family. To a degree you are sensitive about their feelings toward you, and your words are a barometer of your reaction to their emotional consideration for you. It is fortunate that you are well liked, for the Sun-ruled desire as much warmth as they give.

You are a free moral agent and as such you are completely aware of your responsibilities, knowing the effect upon others of every action of your own. You never abuse your social freedom by taking license or liberty with the rights of human beings, which are your rights in full.

This is the portrait of the Ideal You—the self you should be if you claim your rightful heritage. With such endowments, you should now take action to bring them to the fore.

Lay the foundations for real and lasting spiritual freedom by living up to this best self. Begin by keeping this word portrait always in the foreground of your consciousness. Next, look upon yourself as deserving to be called ideal, for, Pythagoras says, "Above all things, reverence yourself."

To recreate yourself in the image of your ideal, do not be content with awareness of your inner strength. Strength is the sturdy quality we see in a steel bridge or a giant tree. It is static. Power is the expression of the strength in action. It is dynamic. So think of how the Ideal You would *act* in every situation, and then act that way.

You have within you infinite wells of power and energy to call upon. With this dynamo at your command, you can create an illumination that will shed light on you, on those you love, and on all those whom you care to favor. Your sense of the absolute and infinite will make you worthy of your ruler, the Sun, and will make "just you" evolve into the Ideal You.

VIRGO: August 23 to September 22.

Most mortals spend much of their lives in wishful thinking. The word "if" and the subjunctive case for conditions contrary to fact are overworked because people express regret over their unfulfilled desires.

Yet there is no need for regret. When you were born, the heavens formed a pattern of your life. This was designed to be the Ideal You. Throughout your childhood few negative influences interfered with your life, and you looked forward confidently to fulfilling the noble framework formed for you.

By now the ways of the world have probably shaken some of that early confidence. The pattern that was to have designed the Ideal You has been distorted. But the natal chart never changes, and therefore you still have within you the ability to become the Ideal You. To aid in this becoming, a blueprint of your ideal self is presented here.

This picture portrays you as you should develop without negative influences to detract from the full expression of your best self. There is no decree of cosmic law that can ever prevent you from growing and improving. For this reason, begin to visualize yourself as your ideal from the beginning of your reading. Fix this picture in your mind as your first step.

Mercury is the planetary ruler of your Sign, Virgo, which represents the concealed fire of the earth. You are quick-moving, love change and variety, but are a stickler for method and order. Since nothing can be accomplished without systematic progression from step to step, it is well that you are endowed with an orderly nature.

You are generous, but not unthinkingly so. Whereas you would never permit anyone you love to suffer want, you are practical enough not to be wasteful, either with your purse or with your love. The reason for this is that you have a delicate sense of balance which adjures the relationship between the spiritual and the material in your character. Harmony must therefore fill the atmosphere that you may breathe it, and you seek to establish it in your environment.

Outwardly you display the same discrimination that exists within. "Neat but not gaudy" Shakespeare might well have said of your attire. The form you have been given to clothe should be well developed. Grace and rhythm distinguish your bodily movements, and an easy charm identifies them.

The magnetism of your personality seems to come from electrical energy generated within you. Yours might be termed a high-frequency ego. The study of the occult intrigues you, and such a pursuit may well work wonders in the development of the Ideal You. Principles that are obscure to others are transparent to you, and you possess a psychic perception that is seemingly uncanny.

Your charm and vivacity in conversation give you popularity, and your good humor enhances it. When anyone makes overtures for your acquaintance, you wish to know his or her character, for you are aware that character is the basis of friendship. Yet you meet all comers courteously, and to each you extend a hearty hand clasp.

A Classic Example of Virgo

The democratic way in which you meet people is but one facet of your expression of faith in the democratic principle. The same fidelity to the people and the country came from the well of patriotism that was the core of the being of Oliver Wendell Holmes. The great professor, author, and physician, father of the Justice of the Supreme Court, was born with the Sun in Virgo, on August 29, 1809.

Holmes displayed the versatility of the natives of your Sign, for he was equally well known as an essayist, poet, teacher, and doctor. It was his first published poem, "Old Ironsides," which saved the historic ship, *The Constitution*, from being scrapped. From this youthful beginning, Dr.

Holmes grew into a literary figure whose pen gave expression to the thoughts and emotions that will always haunt men's minds.

The Ideal You could earn no greater tribute than that which was paid to Holmes by Howells, the literateur and diplomat of the nineteenth century. "He could not be with you a moment without shedding upon you the light of his flashing wit, his radiant humor, and he shone equally upon the rich and poor in mind."

This Virgo poet understood the striving nature of humanity, for in his Secret of the Stars, he speaks of "The climbing soul of man." An innate sympathy with the occult is also shown in his lines:

> The wild swayings of our planet show
> That worlds unseen surround the world we know

With the same understanding, he wrote of Mars as "the foe of human kind," and of Venus as "the celestial charmer."

Courage marks the Ideal You indelibly. You have the bravery and perspicacity to look into your own soul. Holmes had even the honesty to bare his, in a work in which he says, "Let me retrace the record of the years that made me what I am."

To become the Ideal You, study yourself. Rout out from the accumulation of the years the traits, quirks, and habits which do not fit into the portrait you should live up to. Compare each word and act of your present way of life with the acts and words that befit the Ideal You. If the portrait and the actuality mirror each other, your path is clear.

Knowledge is the key to understanding. Action is the key to becoming.

Visualize yourself as the Ideal You. Make every action count as a step toward becoming that self. Use your courage to discount the criticism of hide-bound conventionality. Employ your cosmically endowed love of variety to make a change—for the better! Live up to your own ideal.

No more pithy counsel could be given than that in Oliver Wendell Holmes' *"The Chambered Nautilus:"*
> Build thee more stately mansions, O my soul,
> As the swift seasons roll!
> Leave thy low-vaulted past!
> Let each new temple, nobler than the last,
> Shut thee from heaven with a dome more vast,
> Till thou at length art free,
> Leaving thine outgrown shell by life's unresting sea.

LIBRA: September 23 to October 23

One of the most frequently voiced wishes of humanity is "If only I were a child again and knew what I know now!"

When the Lords of Karma decided it was time for you to make an appearance, you did so.

At that moment, the moment of your birth, you were issued a license to lead an ideal life. This license is your horoscope, the picturization of the pattern formed by the planets and luminaries in the heavens at the time. It enables and qualifies you to live up to the highest characteristics, standards and ideals of your Sign under the governorship of the planet Venus. These endowments comprise the Ideal You.

In the intervening years many changes have taken place.

Emotional experiences and conflicts, social successes and defeats, and economic conquests and failures have all wrought changes in you. Yet your natal chart does not change, and so the Ideal You is still a reality.

You can be the person in the portrait of the Ideal You if you follow these simple guides. Remember that these are the traits endowed upon you by the placement of the Sun in Libra and the governorship by Venus of your Sign. Be conscious always of the existence of these potent innate forces. Pre-test every action by comparing it with the way the Ideal You would behave under the same circumstances.

The symbol of your Sign is the Scales, representing balance, justice and harmony. These comprise an inner law of the universe, forming the invisible bonds which hold together the celestial bodies of the solar system and those in space beyond the ken of man. Mental and emotional balance distinguish you. Righteousness and fairness illumine your conduct. Your sense of harmony brings rhythm, bodily grace and serenity to your way of life.

As Venus is the governing planet of your Sign, you admire beauty, and you can create it. Venus is the planetary ruler of the arts, and many poets, musicians and painters have been born with Venus strong in their horoscopes. You are inspired to eliminate poverty and eradicate ugliness. To this end you devote your natural energy and generous services.

You have a special talent for compensating for any tiny flaw or defect in your individuality. Your aim is to make an ingratiating impression upon everyone. For this reason voice culture and training interest you, and you constantly try to improve your diction and modulate your tonal pitch. Conservative but modern clothes are your choice. You like the best, and you feel it is a good investment to get it rather than to compromise with shoddy, inexpensive substitutes.

You are very sensitive to love. Personal magnetism attracts many people to you, and you respond like the strings of a harp to the touch of the musician.

A Classic Example of Libra

The great qualities of the Libra-born are exemplified in the personality of one simple man who was the spiritual and political leader of millions. The charm, intelligence, intuitive perception, and delightful humor endowed by the planet Venus were the visible and irresistible qualities of Mohandas Karamchand Gandhi, born October 2, 1869.

Ghandi is known as "Mahatma," meaning Great Soul. This name for the man whose word has become scripture to millions arose spontaneously on their lips in response to his great work on behalf of their liberation. He has also been called, and deservedly so, the greatest Indian since Buddha.

The tact, consideration, and magnetism of this Libra-born leader are so well known that his political opponents were warned not to visit him lest they yield to his side. Yet for a principle, the gentle Mahatma could be ruthlessly brutal. For this reason he was called one of the "terrible meek," and was widely known as the most unpretentious of men.

Practitioner of his own philosophy, Ghandi lived in his ashram, clad only in coarse white cloth, in a village inhabited by Untouchables, which caste he tried to raise. He stated that the core of his philosophy was, "The only reform is self--reform." In denying that he was a saint, he averred his essentially religious nature by remarking that God Almighty was his Adviser General and bodyguard.

This is the man who "has changed the face of India, given pride and character to a cringing and demoralized people, and built up strength and consciousness in the masses." Yet, asked what his likes were, he replied, "I like fresh air, children, laughter, friends and the truth." Asked what he disliked most, he said, "A lie."

Ghandi did not become a world figure, a spiritual teacher, or a Great Soul without striving. As late as 1936, he deplored the fact that he had not yet completely vanquished bodily needs and urges. This from the man whose mere threat to fast made a world crisis imminent!

The western world is not the environment in which to try to live the same life as Ghandi. However, he can be—and should be—your inspiration. You have the same potentialities, and you can emulate the life of this great man in the development of the same innate traits. In doing so, you will approach, and perhaps achieve the Ideal You.

This portrait of the Ideal You is your character and personality unsullied by the cares of life. You can attain it only by action, and that action involves work along the lines of self-development. First of all, it requires a courageous honesty on your part with yourself.

You have acquired habits of thought and conduct which probably need to be eradicated. You cannot get rid of them unless you study yourself, discover them, admit you have them, and then work on getting out of the cage of enslavement where they have imprisoned you.

And you must bear in mind at all times the picture of what you can be. Visualize yourself constantly as the person represented in your natal chart—unchanged only in the sense that worldly complications have not set in to throw you off the path of success and happiness.

Next, always act as the Ideal You would act. Do not permit the portrait of yourself to degenerate as did the fictional portrait of Dorian Grey. Every word you utter can add to the grace of the voice and lips that speak it. Every gesture can add to the nobility of your hands. Every thought can enhance the poise of the mind when it issues.

You will not only live a joyous life in reaching for this ideality; you will be building a better future life.

SCORPIO: October 24 to November 22

There is a tenet of Universal Law which is usually the first one learned by the student of occult subjects: *As above, so below.*

Scholars and initiates have meditated upon this simple yet profound phrase for many ages as mankind counts time. The implication of these four words is your applicable cosmic ally. Seers have applied it to the interpretation of events upon this planet. Philosophers have applied it to the conduct of mankind. Meteorologists have applied it to our gales and storms.

It applies to you! As above, so below. The cosmic law includes you in its operation. Above, at the time of your birth, the stars, the luminaries and the planets formed a picture. This celestial blueprint might have required the speediest of all cameras to be photographed. Yet for the instant that it was captured on the plate, the heavens formed a picture of the Ideal You.

Below, as life coursed through your newly emancipated body, rejoicing took place. You were the focal point of the vibratory rays of each of the heavenly bodies as they reached the geographical spot where you were born. The potentialities of greatness were brought to life.

That picture of the skies is your horoscope, and it represents you as you were meant to be. Since then so much happened that you may not fully recognize a complete interpretation of your chart. Or you might regretfully ask your astrologer, "What has happened to me?"

Time and circumstances have dimmed, faded, or erased the picture of the Ideal You. But your natal chart never changes, and so you can refresh your mind with the portrait of the Ideal You presented here.

You possess a power of persistency which amounts to indomitable will. You can become anything you choose to be. Indefatigable in your efforts, you always manage to achieve your aims, both immediate and distant. In matters of improving humanity, you are a leader. You have seen the light on the path, and your enthusiasm stimulates you to enlighten others. Your power is balanced by kindness, and your force by gentleness.

Scorpio is the middle Sign of the water triplicity. This gives you a love of sea views and of ocean travel. It also makes you fond of lakes, rivers, and brooks. On the waters when viewing their charming scenery, you feel at home, and a sensation of great contentment comes over you.

In appearance and manner you are the acme of dignity. There is an air of serenity about you which inspires confidence and admiration. Your courtesy and affability are such that you are always treated with respect. Show and display are alien to your nature, but you are fond of the fine things on the material plane. For this reason you are a model of good taste in clothing, home decoration, and the arts.

One of your distinguishing characteristics is your eloquence. The spoken and written word are tools which you employ with the skill of genius. You show both taste and tact in your choice of words. This use of your vocabulary, combined with a well-modulated voice, gives you the power to influence those with whom you communicate. Your influence in gaining your high aims is widespread. You can well apply this talent with the use of words to do editorial work, exposition, and creative writing of a high imaginative quality.

Pluto is the governing planet of your Sign. Many potential powers rest within you for this reason. Surgery is a field in which many who have the Sun in Scorpio succeed. The governing planet also endows cool courage on you, and in emergencies you fully understand the necessity for being calm and for acting rather than being hysterical.

Pluto is the planet of conversion. It enables you to transform things. Under the influence of its vibratory rays, you can change ideas into realities, aspirations into achievements, and hopes into realizations. You can put your innate qualities into daily use in advancing your ambitions, in ameliorating social conditions, and in healing the troubles of a suffering society.

A Classic Example of Scorpio

Mrs. Gertrude Atherton, one of the first American woman novelists to achieve world fame, was born under the Sign Scorpio on October 30, 1857. The eloquence typical of Scorpio was hers; during her lifetime she wrote some 40 books.

The indomitable spirit of Scorpio is manifested in all her works. She objected strenuously to the hidebound tenets of convention which she satirically exposed in her works, conducting, as her obituary stated, "a fifty-year war against Mrs. Grundy."

The good taste of the Scorpio-born is reflected in her love of serious literature for which she developed a liking at the age of fourteen. She also manifested Scorpio's love of water in the many voyages she made abroad.

Mrs. Atherton was a living example of the persistency of those born with Mars as their co-ruling planet. It took her four years to find a publisher for her first book, and in all that time she never allowed herself to become discouraged. As she herself stated, more than fifty years after the publication of that first book, "I shall remark here only that any career is a fight from start to finish, and needs as much will power and courage as talent." In the true spirit of the Pluto-ruled, she goes on to say, "But it would not be half so interesting otherwise. As to development, that goes on insensibly from year to year."

All social strata interested Gertrude Atherton. She tried to improve humanity not only by satirizing its foolish faults in her writings, but by rendering active service in civic affairs. She served on many committees in San Francisco, lending the advantages of her culture and exquisite taste to work designed to improve civic beauty and to further education.

The universal viewpoint of Scorpio is shown in her words, "I abominate 'isms.'" The practical idealism of her view is proved in her statement, "I am quite willing to admit that our form of government is far from perfect, but want something better, not worse."

Her epitaph might well be taken from the words in her autobiography, "I prize liberty and freedom."

Such is the portrait of the Ideal You and a vivid example of those traits which distinguish you. With your cosmic heritage of a brilliant, supple brain and an enormous capacity for work, you may live up to the portrait.

Bear this picture of yourself—as you might be—always in mind. Visualize your way of life and conduct all times. Evaluate the worthiness of your every act before you do it, of your every word before you speak it. If it is not worthy of your highest self, discard it.

Thus you can grow into the image of what has been designed for you above. Live up to this portrait of yourself, and you will become the Ideal You—here below. Remember, *As above, so below.*

SAGITTARIUS: November 23 to December 21

The fall of the year is somehow a season of introspection. When the loveliness of nature fades, mankind is disposed to look back upon the springtime. Let the season of your birth be your invitation to look back upon those times generally referred to as "the best days of your life." Have you ever cogitated on why those days of the past were the best days? The answer is that your ideals, ambitions and desires all seemed within easy reach.

You were in a state of unspoiled innocence that was the Ideal You. The tar brush of tawdry experience and the bitterness of disappointment had not touched you. Since then you have lived through what the Romans called the "Dog Days."

When you were born, a horoscope erected would have made a design of your endowments as reflected from the pattern of the stars, the planets and the luminaries. Most important of all, the Sun was in Sagittarius. That blueprint is a design which outlines and delineates the Ideal You.

Why are you no longer the image of that Ideal You? Circumstances, emotions, finances, economics, world crisis—all have taken their toll. But more important than the dear price paid in the school of experience is the fact that you may once more be the Ideal You.

By visualizing yourself constantly in the role of your best self and by living according to the superior standards of your innate traits, you can actually build your character and personality up to the inherent potentialities with which you were born.

Astrology reconstructs the portrait of the Ideal You. Study the analysis of your potentialities presented here, and then make a strenuous effort to live up to it. Apply yourself and your powers of concentration to the most worthwhile task in life, the development of your highest ideals.

Your Sign, the last of the Fire triplicity, has as its symbol the Archer, representing the high and noble aspirations toward which you strive. Therefore you know how and what to aim at, and you generally hit the mark. You are progressive, enterprising and far-seeing. As a rule, you can tell how an idea or project will work out at its very inception. When you rely upon your own opinions and intuition, you can attain success.

You possess much wisdom, a great deal of which has been culled from psychic power. The realm of prophecy is yours to roam, and many of your Sign are natural clairvoyants. You search the whole universe with your mind while your unique insight enables you to see what others fail to understand.

Your talents are many and varied. However, your versatility does not impel you to scatter your abilities; for you can concentrate on one thing at a time until the task in hand is completed perfectly. You are decided and positive about every venture in which you are interested, and the energy and activity you pour into it often cause other people to marvel at you.

Jupiter is the governing planet of Sagittarius, and you are fortunate indeed to have "the Great Benefic" as the strongest influence in your horoscope. You know the way to market, and you know the way to save. The good things of life are not doled out to you, but are yours in abundance. It is your nature to be careful about money matters, but not close or penurious. Knowing the value of money, you believe in setting some aside for future benefits and pleasures. However, you are the first and the most generous with your help when it comes to relieving distress or suffering.

To your associates, you display a strong and honest nature. The magnetism of your personality seems to endow you with almost hypnotic powers, and you attract a host of friends. Your eloquence makes your words strike home, for you deal only in the truth and what you say has great effect. When you enter the lists in the cause of right and justice, no stronger champion could be found. You deplore humbug and valiantly battle in the crusade for truth.

A Classic Example of Sagittarius

One of the noblest protagonists of truth was Samuel Langhorne Clemens, born under Sagittarius on November 30, 1835, and known universally and affectionately as "Mark Twain." He was an outspoken, robust character, and the most loved American of his time.

The creator of Tom Sawyer and Huckleberry Finn was a

fearless fighter in his serious moods. Before the establishment of the copyright laws, authors—he among them—suffered the loss of their royalties through the piracy of publishers. Mark Twain crusaded for the protection of the income of writers, and appeared before the Congressional Committee where his impassioned speech had a sensational effect. He was strongly opposed to the coolie wages being paid American laborers and waged a battle for higher pay. His friend Howells said, "His mind and soul were with those who do the hard work of the world in fear of those who employ them and underpay them all they can."

Like all Sagittarians, Mark Twain was close to the people. He populated his books with characters of the new West, and the South, but he satirized almost bitterly the traditional culture of New England. The sympathy and compassion of the Sagittarius-born was one of his outstanding traits. It was said of him that "Nothing could have been wiser, nothing tenderer than his humanity, which was not for humanity alone. It sickened him even to see a blackbird shot down." His closeness to the common man was demonstrated when he said that he was just as proud of the praise of the porter in his hotel in Vienna as that of the German Emperor.

Found in an error, Mark Twain was the readiest of men to admit it. He was the most caressing of men in his pity. When he gave a command, whether it was to one of his children or to a servant, it was the softest of entreaties.

Sagittarius is a Sign of eloquence. Mark Twain was one of the most prolific of writers, his complete works filling a whole shelf in the library. He was a master of narrative, style and construction. Yet with all his written composition, he became the most consummate public performer of his time. He was a practiced speaker, every one of his lectures being a sell-out, and he derived a huge income from these public appearances.

One could easily detect the powerful influence of the planet Jupiter in Mark Twain's horoscope. He was prosperous, and he showed it. He loved magnificence, good food, and dramatic clothing. Although he lived in a mansion, he detested the vain ceremony of knocking on doors and ringing bells. His was the happiest of households, and though the hair on his great shaggy head was white, his beloved wife always called him by his pet name, "Youth."

No matter what your own age might be, you can earn the name of Youth by embodying its spirit. This is the portrait of the Ideal You untouched by the hand of time. It is the essential and indomitable you, which you can become by putting your mind on becoming it.

CAPRICORN: December 22 to January 19

It was William Shakespeare who said that we should "hold the mirror up to nature." To understand your own nature, you should hold the mirror up to it. However, few people, even those with deep appreciative powers, have the clarity of vision to see their own natures in their true light. It is the function of Astrology and has been for countless ages to interpret the natal charts of people for their own benefit.

Your horoscope at the time of your birth mirrored your every quality, your every potentiality. It was the Ideal You. Hold the mirror up to your nature now. The image it reflects is dimmed, has flaws, seems vague here and glaring there. What is the reason for the change? One reason is that growth means change, another is that contacts with the outside world inevitably take a toll upon the ideality that was essentially you.

However, you must realize that your natal chart never changes. For that reason, you can still attain and demonstrate every potentiality with which you were endowed at birth. In other words, by extending the effort, thought, and will it requires, you can still become the Ideal You!

You are presented here with an image of the Ideal You, born under the Sign Capricorn. With the will power at your command, wipe away the dust and shadows gathered through the years which obscure this image. See yourself as you are in this picture. Visualize yourself at all times as the person you were meant to be, and always act as that ideal would. Weigh every word before you utter it; consider every act before you perform it. You now have a standard by which you can measure, so use it to evaluate everything you do. Veto anything not worthy of the Ideal You, and you will see its image gradually emerge from the dim portrait of the present.

No reward comes without effort. You must concentrate your desire and thought upon this achievement. In addition to the efforts you make on your own behalf, you should ask for help from Him from whom all things flow. It is no sin to ask for success. The Divine Plan included your birth at the precise time that took place. At the time the heavens formed a pattern which heralded your rebirth. The Plan included you, and you may include the Pattern-Maker in your prayers and meditations. Ask that you may live up to the design cut out for you, that you may image the Ideal You.

It has been said that your Sign, Capricorn, last Sign of the Earth triplicity, is "the mysterious Sign of the Earth, and within it is the occult side of history."

At least one side of your nature craves solitude and seeks

meditation. You like study and deep thinking, while all superficial things fail to appeal to you. Your admiration of the intellect knows no bounds, and you are tireless in your efforts to cultivate your mind.

Although you are a hard worker, you are sometimes stymied because you try to do too many things at once. Greatness can be yours once you have learned the lesson of concentrating on one thing.

The solitude of the Capricornian, symbolized by the lone goat on the mountain top, represents your own spirit of independence, as well as your policy of non-interference in the lives of other individuals. Your most splendid achievements are directed to the furtherance of your own career.

Innate wisdom makes you philosophical. Should a depressing mood assail you, you know how to dissipate it by calling upon the knowledge and power that are intuitively yours. In the same way, you can be a joy, a boon, a comfort and a solace to others, for you have as deep a sympathy for the sufferings of humanity as the Man of Sorrows whose Sign was thought to have been Capricorn according to our modern, corrected calendar.

You have a magnetic quality that attracts people to you, and in public life you can create an almost hypnotic effect with your control of the public or an audience. You hold your friends dear and fast, and you are very discriminating in choosing them. You are sensitive to their feelings, and once you are hurt, it takes long for you to get over it.

Your generosity knows no bounds. No appeal to your purse goes unanswered if there is any help you can provide. In business dealings, you have a broad outlook; you cannot be petty, nor can you tolerate pettiness in others.

Harmony and beauty are necessary to your spiritual happiness. Metaphysics and occult science appeal to you very strongly, and the study of these subjects not only increases your general fund of knowledge, but gives you a philosophy of life that you can always call upon.

The desire of the Capricorn-born to improve the general state of humanity has produced many great teachers and statesmen in this Sign. It is also the Sign of the government, and much of the administrative detail work of nations is executed by Capricorn natives.

A Classic Example of Capricorn

Alfred Emanuel Smith's career has been rather typical of the Capricorn-born. He was born in New York City, on December 30, 1873, in humble circumstances. He rose from the sidewalks of New York to the governorship of his native state, and to even higher eminence in running for the presidency of the nation.

The spiritual side of Capricorn is expressed in this great statesman in the religiosity of his nature. He was one of the most eminent of Catholic laymen.

The humanitarian outlook of Capricorn came into active play when Smith was governor of New York. Under his guidance the lot of the workman was indeed improved. Social legislation provided insurance, compensation, and regulation of the working hours of women and children was put into effect. There was not a resident of his state who did not in some way benefit by the many terms of office to which "Al" was elected.

Capricornians, however, are not mere dreamers. There is a

practical side to your nature. Alfred E. Smith was not only an executive of many important corporations, he was the typical climber of your Sign. The goat on the mountain top being the symbol of your Sign, was it not to have been expected that a Capricornian like Al Smith, of humble birth, should build the tallest structure in the entire world—the Empire State Building?

Your Sign is under the governorship of the planet Saturn, "the Cosmic Timekeeper." Many are the lessons you will learn during this incarnation. One of them can be your living up to the high potentialities with which you were endowed at birth.

Keep this picture of the Ideal You always in mind, and never stray from its standards. You can be the standard-bearer for a better world. Yours is the power to climb, and you should reach the heights attainable to the Ideal You.

AQUARIUS: January 20 to February 18

The highest aspirations of man are his ideals. Striving toward the accomplishment of these ideals is man's way of seeking the Image in which he was made, for occult philosophy teaches that we are all gods in the becoming.

This process of "becoming" takes the form of evolving from one incarnation to another. At your birth, you have every innate quality needed to attain the ideal state during this incarnation. Your path of progress, the road up to self-realization, is heralded in the skies by the beautiful pattern formed by the planets and the luminaries which Astrology calls your horoscope.

Yet, rare indeed is the individual who has attained every

one of his early aspirations. The complexity of life today usually detracts from the fulfilling of your hopes. But you can still do it and become the Ideal You.

Astrology has retained the portrait of the Ideal You which you yourself may have mislaid. A picture of the Ideal You is presented here, based upon your Sun Sign and its governing planet. Study this word image. Keep it always in your mind. Live up to it by doing only what this ideal would do, and you will *become* the Ideal You.

You who were born under Aquarius, the last Sign of the Air triplicity, have more power to make of yourself what you choose than most people born under any other Sign.

Your role in the cosmic drama is that of the healer. You can bring consolation to the sick and weary, and solace to the bereaved. The words you use seem to go from your lips to the very heart of your auditor, bringing joy where misery once reigned.

Activity and industry characterize your nature. Yours is a twenty-four hour day, and you would actually be on the go all that time if the physical body did not require rest. Regardless of the branch of industry, science, or art in which you are interested, you have the necessary qualities to succeed. In fact, it is typical of your Sign to make a success of more than one business, interest, or hobby at the same time.

One of the principles to which you strictly adhere is freedom from obligation. You know that debts are the impediments which hold you back on the road to success, and you therefore discharge your responsibilities the moment they fall due.

So sensitive are you that your mentality might be compared to a photographic plate. You rarely have to memorize facts, figures or faces, for they make a lasting impression from your first view of them. For this reason you command a great many facts, much information, and an infinite number of impressions. This capacity makes you a "quick study," as you seemingly absorb the things to be learned with almost no conscious effort.

You rarely display ill temper, being calm, quiet, and peaceful. You emanate serenity so that not only can you work in an atmosphere where others would be distracted, but you help to establish restfulness.

Frequently you possess divinatory powers which surprise those who know you. The magnetism which accompanies this force brings you many friends and admirers. Approval of your ideas and suggestions comes even from people who do not know you very well, but who are attracted by the truth and logic of what you say. You are attracted to philosophy and occultism, and deep study in these fields can produce from your innate interests a profound scholar of "the secrets behind the veil."

Your Sign has always been illustrious because those born under the governorship of the planet Uranus have had the public welfare at heart. Every classic of Astrology praises the interest of Aquarians in improving the general welfare of humanity. Sometimes you devote yourself to the public interest more deeply than to your own affairs or those of your loved ones. Occultly speaking, this is the highest and noblest form of unselfishness.

A Classic Example of Aquarius

Probably the most renowned figure born under Aquarius is Abraham Lincoln. How apt is the poet's description of him:

>A homely hero born of star and sod;
>A Peasant Prince; a Masterpiece of God.
>(Walter Malone, *Abraham Lincoln*)

He came into the world on February 12, 1809, in a log cabin in Kentucky—a cabin still standing, the center of a beautiful national shrine at Hodgenville, in his native state.

What does this giant of humaneness not represent to the entire universe? As the typical Aquarian rising to the greatest heights, through the exertion of his innate forces he became the ideal of American democracy—the poor boy of humble parentage, lacking every advantage of environment, who yet became the President of the United States.

The truly remarkable memory, photographic in nature, of the Aquarian-born was another trait of Lincoln's. Impressed by the pure logic of geometry and the simple steps of reasoning thereof—which can, of course, be applied to any subject or debate—he went directly to the source. He memorized the entire *Elements of Euclid*.

Here was a truly universal man. The physical, mental and spiritual qualities of his makeup blended into the great humanitarian with perfect balance. The rail-splitter, the scholar, the lawyer, the statesman, the tactician, the diplomat, and God-loving individual, the husband, the father, and the great humorist all dwelt within the same human frame—an enormous frame it had to be to contain so much man, so many men.

Little need be said of the unselfishness of Abraham Lincoln. It is an axiom that he died for the humane principles for which he lived, that he was a martyr for a cause, and that the cause succeeded.

Lincoln never compromised. He knew no middle path. Indeed he considered it vain even to look for one. As he said himself, in the concluding sentence of his great address delivered at Cooper Union, for which he won national acclaim, "Let us have faith that right makes might; and in that faith let us to the end dare to do our duty as we understand it."

This is an example of the ideal Aquarian, born under the same Sign as you. Lincoln was a man who fulfilled his destiny, who represented the highest attributes of your astrological Sign.

Not everyone born under the same Sign can be another Lincoln, but you can fulfill your destiny and live up to the highest ideals of your Sign.

Bear in mind the noble principles with which you are endowed. Then live up to them. The living up to them will then become a step in the becoming.

Only your own desire and initiative can make you what you want to be. Keep the light of the Luminaries ever shining on the portrait of the Ideal You. Follow the road map of the stars to the attainment of fulfilling your highest aspirations. Think of yourself as the Ideal You, *act* according to the principles of the Ideal You, and in the course of progress you will evolve into the Ideal You.

PISCES: February 19 to March 20

Plato taught that before creation there existed certain types of ideal models, of which ideas or created objects are the visible images. An idea can be seen in operation. The ideal, it follows, seems to be preconceived.

Before your entrance into the world at the time of your birth, the Lords of Karma had created an ideal model of you. The herald of this ideal was the design created in the heavens by the planets, constellations and the Luminaries, and called your horoscope.

As you grew up into this pattern, awareness of externals began to come to you. From year to year, the attachment to your parents grew into love. Intellectual curiosity led you abroad, and you widened your circle of acquaintances, and broadened the sphere of your knowledge. You wanted the best of everything, and you wanted the best for everyone.

However, as you buffeted the realities of life, an element of discouragement entered. As you tried to attain unselfish aspirations and discovered obstacles all along the path, an element of cynicism entered your personality and outlook.

One might say, "There *went* the Ideal You"—except that the model of which you are the image can never be destroyed. For this reason, you can still become the Ideal You, and therefore, the model is presented to you here.

Visualize yourself as the person in this word picture. This is the first step toward attainment. Have faith that you will grow to be the living representation of this portrait. Affirm daily that you are becoming the mirror of this ideality. In your meditations, dwell upon your evolution into the Ideal You.

Pisces is the twelfth, or last Sign of the Zodiac. Occult tradition holds that each incarnation finds one born in the Sign following that of the previous incarnation. You are therefore presumed to have completed one round of the cycles of life and may contemplate the satisfaction that accompanies completion, as well as look forward to new beginnings on a higher level.

Yours is the Sign of occultism. Just as the zodiacal symbol of Pisces represents two fish, one going upstream and the other down, there are magnetic forces at your command which go in two directions at the same time. You can be the receptor of telepathic sendings, and you can charge the atmosphere with dynamic messages.

Metaphysics, Astrology, and philosophy intrigue you profoundly. Many leading thinkers along these lines and many spiritualist mediums have been born under the Sign Pisces. Your interest in these subjects is far from superficial, nor is it the manifestation of mere intellectual curiosity. Your nature is too deeply religious to delve into these matters for entertainment, for spiritually you are a giant with potent forces and dynamic powers at your command.

There are depths of love within your nature which are more profound than those found in any other Sign. This emotion is all pervading, extending to nature, all of its citizens, and all humanity. You are naturally noble and generous, and motivated by desire to help the needy.

You are sensitive to the desires and inner natures of other people, and you put yourself out to please them. Self-sacrifice is one of your outstanding traits—to the extent that you seem to be indifferent to your own wants. To you the words, "It is more blessed to give than to receive" are no mere cant; they form the legend on the heraldic crest of Pisces.

You have a reputation for honesty, and your name is a synonym for trustworthiness. You also put the same faith in others that they have in you. Loyalty is the handmaiden to your every thought.

The trident of Neptune, symbol of your governing planet, represents your innate versatility. The beauty in art is your creation and the object of your admiration. You are fond of the static as well as the dynamic arts—painting, sculpture, literature, and music give you sensual and intellectual pleasures.

A Classic Example of Pisces

The brilliant versatility of the Neptune-ruled has no greater nor more classic example than George Washington, born February 22, 1732, at ten o'clock in the morning, in the Virginia family mansion that had already housed four generations of American Washingtons. The versatility of George Washington leaves almost no individual epithet by which to classify or characterize him. He was noted as: surveyor, soldier, gentleman-farmer, expert in animal husbandry, law-giver, "Father of his Country," President, Commander-in-Chief, even—in Piscean fashion, according to some—lover.

And truly Piscean and Neptune-ruled, he was. Washington did not seek the War for Independence any more than any American has sought a war since then. He rendered his services, not for self-aggrandizement nor reward, but for the benefit of his fellow men. This is clearly brought out in a letter he wrote in 1776, wherein his reference to keeping above water is rather apt for one born in the last Sign of the Water triplicity: "If I am able to keep above water in the esteem of mankind, I shall feel myself happy. If I did not consult the *public good,* more than my own tranquility, I should long ere this have put everything to the cast of a die."

Thomas Jefferson described Washington as having a great, powerful mind and sounder judgment than anyone else. This is characteristic of those born under Pisces. He was incapable of fear, meeting personal danger with the calmest unconcern. Once he made up his mind, he carried out his decisions no matter what obstacles opposed.

Washington's integrity was very pure, and his justice inflexible. No motives of interest or consanguinity, of friendship or hatred, could bias his decision. He was a wise, a good, and a great man. His wisdom and experience helped him to overcome the high temper of the Piscean because he had learned how tremendous was his wrath when it broke its bonds.

The first President was held in the highest esteem by his contemporaries. Jefferson, who was perhaps closer to him than anyone else, said of him, "Never did nature and fortune combine more perfectly to make a man great, and to place him in the same constellation (sic) with whatever worthies have merited from man an everlasting remembrance."

You who were born under the Sign Pisces share the natural dignity and grace which distinguished Washington. The urbanity within is expressed in your free carriage. Natural and spontaneous politeness add charm to your presence.

This is the picture of the Ideal You, as designed in the blueprint of the heavens at the time of your birth. You can become this noble personage if you will act to do so. Bear this picture always in your mind. Act as the person in the portrait would act, for that person is you.

Your natal chart never changes, so live up to its best aspects, and you will evolve into the Ideal You.

The Decans on an Egyptian temple of the
1st Century B.C.

Arabian version of the Zodiac, 9th Century

A unique example of a Chinese Zodiac,
10th Century

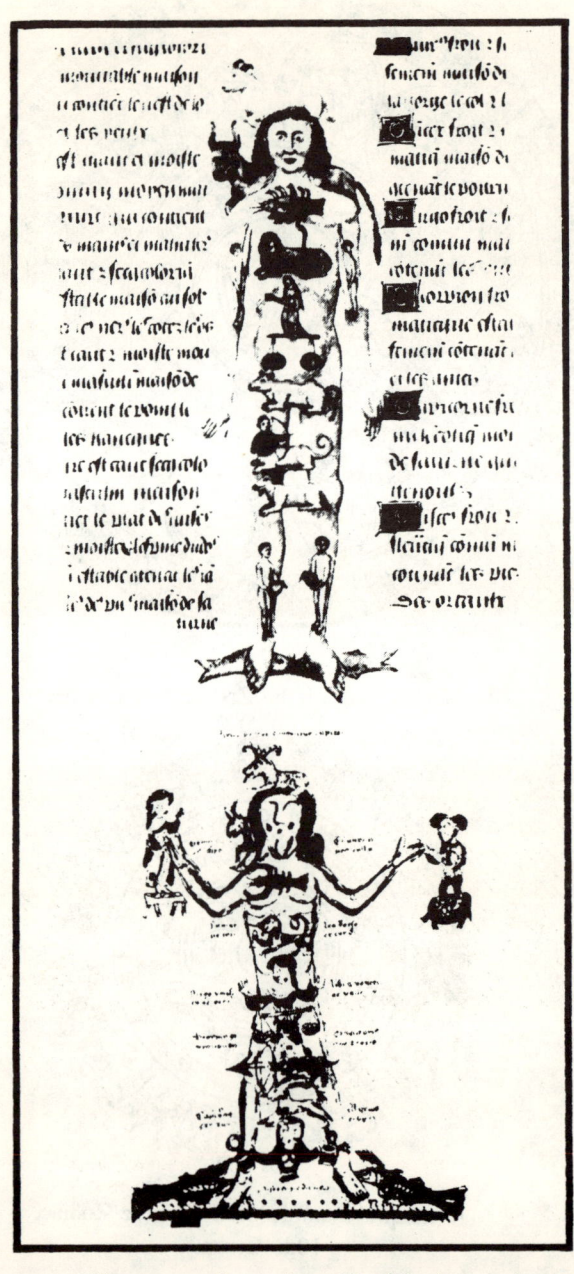

Figures used to time blood-letting and operations

Square type of horoscope showing the Man
of the Zodiac

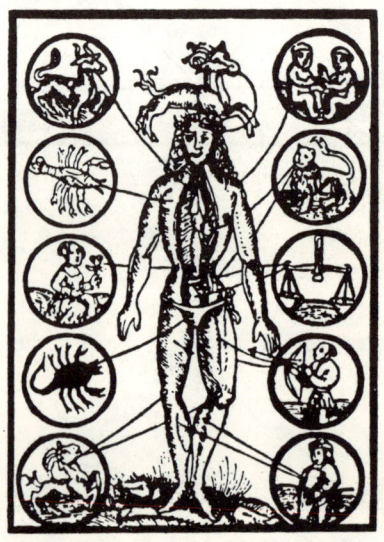

Examples of the Zodiac Man used in the
diagnosis and treatment of disease

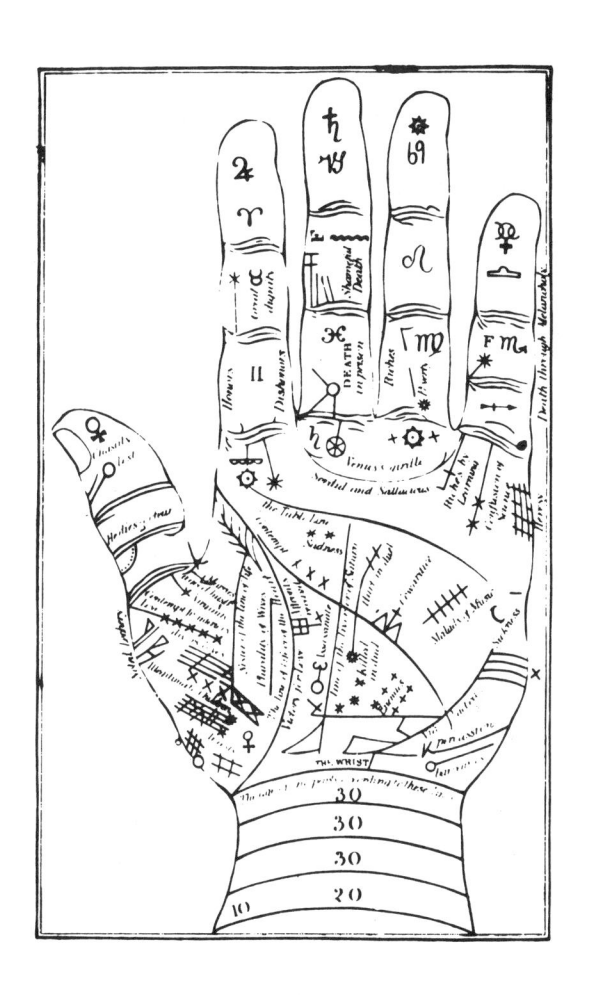

The human hand showing the astrological
rulers of each segment

Old French planetary symbols

Page of a 16th Century English calendar showing Mercury
and his children

A 16th Century representation of Arabian astrologers

Nostradamus, 16th Century French astrologer-physician to royalty. His predictions are still studied today.

A 16th Century Venetian astrologer

A 16th Century design of a horoscope

Bael, said to be the "familiar" of
Nostradamus

William Lilly, famous 17th Century English astrologer

A 17th Century astrologer casting a horoscope

A French 17th Century drawing showing
the Signs ruling various parts of the body
and organs

Chapter IV

THE POWER OF YOUR PERSONALITY

The Story of Each Decan

To understand the Decan, you may visualize in your mind's eye the statement in the Bible, "In my Father's House there are many mansions."

The Zodiac, or belt of the heavens as you see it, is divided into twelve equal segments, each of which is a Sign. You were born under the Sign in which the Sun was placed at the time of your birth.

Now, if you visualize each Sign of the Zodiac as a House, you can also picture the house as having three stories.

If you were born while the Sun was shining on the first floor or story, that would correspond to the first ten degrees of the Sign, which is called the First Decan.

If you were born while the Sun was in the second ten degrees of the Sign, as it might on the second floor or story, then you were automatically a member of the Second Decan of that same Sign.

If you were born while the Sun was in the sector of the Sign from its 21st to 30th degrees, then you belong to the Third Decan, as though you were born on the third floor of the house with the Sun then shining into it.

The Sun remains in each of these ten degree segments or portions about ten days. It is as though it shines on each floor of the three story house for about ten days.

The House is always the same, but is divided into floors for further understanding of the Solar influence on it.

For this reason, the illumination from the Sun has a special significance, for it lights up the portion of the house you were in at birth. And the portion of the house is known in Astrology as the Decan.

Since there are twelve zodiacal Signs, and each is divided into three equal parts, you will find the explanation of 36 Decans in the delineations given below. Look for the Decan that gives the date on which you were born or the dates between which you were born. It is a simple matter to find your own Decan, as all you need do is find your birth date in the list of Decans.

The Decan delineation given here is a more specific interpretation because it narrows you down to the smaller section of the chart in which the Sun was located at your birth. In addition, you will find the keyword to your Decan, the Planetary

Ruler of your Decan, or its auxiliary Ruler, and the constellation of your Decan.

The ruling constellations are interesting mythological features since these star clusters are no longer in the place in the skies that they were in at the time such rulerships were assigned thousands of years ago. However, even the dictionary still defines constellations as, "your character or disposition as determined by the stars."

To understand yourself better, read carefully the delineation for your Decan. Of course, this chapter includes all the Decans, so you can also get insight into the character of your acquaintances, friends, and relatives.

As you read your Decan delineation which tells your constellation, think of the words of the famous poet, Gower, who wrote:

"It is constellation which causeth all that a man doeth."

ARIES DECANATES

First Decan: March 21st to March 31st Birthdays.
Planetary Ruler: Mars. Keyword: Initiative.
Constellation: Cassiopeia, a beautiful woman seated upon a throne at the left of a king whose crown is made of stars, and whose scepter is inclined toward her.

Your mentality is keen, alert, and ever active. The executive is the role you desire to perform in the play of life. There is wide scope to your thinking which sneers at all things petty and tawdry. So well defined is your sense of values that anyone who knows you never tries to pawn off the shoddy or make-shift on you. Your ability to co-ordinate and complete work is outstanding. Although you dislike to compromise, you know how to adapt yourself to almost any demands. You need no artificial props to attract attention or to make you popular. Independence of spirit reduces your requirements for social approbation and the self-same independence brings you the admiration of truly worthwhile and thinking friends.

Second Decan: April 1st to April 10th Birthdays.
Zodiacal Ruler: Sun. Keyword: Leadership.
Constellation: The sea monster bound to a pair of fish, and being led by the Lamb.

Constructive and creative abilities put you far to the front of the crowd, which recognizes the validity of your position there. The whole-hearted fervor which you inject into everything you do makes the rest of the group glad and willing to follow you. Since you are efficient and conscientious, you are capable of managing a home and a job at the same time. Your taste is for the best alone, and this applies to all things: material, spiritual, and human relations. You are essentially an idealist, and can worship at but one shrine, perfection. There must be mutual respect for you to enjoy mutual love, and you will never be satisfied until it is yours.

Third Decan: April 11th to April 19th Birthdays.
Planetary Ruler: Jupiter. Keyword: Foresight.
Constellation: Perseus, a vigorous male, with winged feet, one of them in the Milky Way, and his head helmeted, with a victor's sword above it.

An almost uncanny prophetic vision enables you to come straight to the point in your efforts and speech. Your confidence in your foreknowledge makes you capable of tackling the most abstruse and complicated problems with complete assurance. It enhances your intuitive shrewdness so that you may succeed in any career to which you aspire. You fully understand the value of money, as a commodity of exchange and as the basis for security in modern economics. In the home, business, or in the world of banking, you can take up a position of trust and retain it for as long as you wish. Your resourcefulness is almost without limit, and it gains you no enemies because you display it with sensible modesty.

TAURUS DECANATES

First Decan: April 20th to April 30th Birthdays.
Planetary Ruler: Venus. Keyword: Affability.

Constellation: Orion, heavenly huntsman, holding his club in one hand and the pelt of a slain lion in the other; girdled by a belt of stars, sword bound therein, he holds one foot aloft as if he is crushing an enemy with it.

The drama, the graphic arts, and music have a tremendous appeal for you. Devoted to the expression and appreciation of these gratifying forms, you are yet sympathetic to every call for help. Whenever there is a distress signal in your environment, you are ready to sacrifice time, money, and your services for the relief of the needy and the sick. Every drive for funds to relieve suffering, and every project to help those in dire straits either at home or abroad is aided cheerfully by you. Your sociability, friendliness, and generous help constitute the type of benevolence that is welcomed. You are dependable, with a multitude of ideas available in your mind for ready use, so that should one fail, you have another to replace it.

Second Decan: May 1st to May 11th Birthdays.
Planetary Ruler: Mercury. Keyword: Organization.
Constellation: Eridanus, a long, winding river symbolizing eternal justice.

You possess a splendid combination of qualities for the role of an executive—you are a worker and an organizer. Whether you are posted in the home, in a business, or some creative field, these qualifications should put you in a position to start important things, operate them efficiently, and carry them to success. You radiate enthusiasm and optimism, two contagious sparks that light the flame of cooperation. Confidence is your sword, and hopefulness your shield. The weary lean on you, the discouraged follow you, and the unhappy seek to emulate you. In areas where eloquence is vital, you might win fame, such as in the fields of playwriting, lecturing, teaching, and politics. You have insight enough not to try to overreach your goal, usually a sure indication that you will attain it.

Third Decan: May 12th the May 20th Birthdays.
Planetary Ruler: Saturn. Keyword: Determination.
Constellation: Auriga, the shepherd protecting his flock.

You have the courage to face facts, even when they are unpleasant. Rationalizing or hiding behind a false veil of security is alien to your nature. When you believe in a cause, it can have no stronger proponent than you. Sentimentality seems a weak trait to you, and you make every effort to rout it or its symptoms out of your system. However, this does not apply to true feelings or the deeper emotions, for when you are touched by a valid cause or experience truly warm emotions, you devote the same active attention to them as to other projects which have gained your interest. You have confidence in yourself, but are well aware that strength lies in unity, and you prefer partnership or collaboration to individual effort. A bit on the stern side, you accept few modifications and no excuses.

GEMINI DECANATES

First Decan: May 21st to May 31st Birthdays.
Planetary Ruler: Mercury. Keyword: Conscientiousness.

Constellation: Lepus, the hare, symbolical of the weaker creature outwitting the stronger.

A faculty for prompt decisions and an ability to direct others qualify you for an executive position in life. Your acts are colored by boldness and dash. Those who know you are aware of your generosity, fondness for doing good, and dependability. When matters of importance arise, you are seldom on the erring side if you follow your inspiration. However, you sometimes go to such extremes in the execution of your duties that you burn up nervous energy and expend vital force. Being meticulous in dress and appearance yourself, you want to see the same in those you associate with, and for this you choose persons of wit and refinement. Diplomatic affairs interest you, and your abilities should give you a voice in them.

Second Decan: June 1st to June 11th Birthdays.
Planetary Ruler: Venus. Keyword: Serenity.

Constellation: Sirius, the great dog, whose name is a derivative of the word meaning victorious prince.

Your nature responds to beauty and harmony, and you manifest your love for both by an active interest in art and music. Distant places with romantic names fascinate you, and you would like to spend much time in travel so that you could visit them. Because you are sensitive to the opinions and feelings of others, you so conduct your life that you win the approval of persons whose respect you value and whose approbation you respect. When you are faced with a problem, you try to fathom it to the depths objectively, leaving the personal and selfish elements out. Because of your unselfish nature, you try to eliminate personal advantage from your dealings. Difficulties hold no terror for you because your reasoning is balanced and your intuition keen. Where there is a way out at all, you will find it.

Third Decan: June 12th to June 20th Birthdays.
Planetary Ruler: Uranus. Keyword: Reason.
Constellation: Canus Minor, or the smaller dog, standing for triumph of reason.

You are interested in people, but your interest is tempered by a rational attitude toward them so that they do not impose on you nor you on them. Familiarity with your friends and family is the limit to which you allow yourself to go in human relations. With all other people, you act with the respect due them, and as a result, they are never rude to you. As an optimist, you see the brighter side of life; and as a realist, you do not delude yourself by insisting that there is no evil in the world. You do your share to spread happiness, but knowing that the only true happiness comes from within, you try to educate and promote people and ideology so that others will do things for themselves.

CANCER DECANATES

First Decan: June 21st to July 2nd Birthdays.
Zodiacal Ruler: Moon. Keyword: Philanthropy.
Constellation: The little bear whose distance from the Earth symbolizes the distant goals and ideals of man.

You are intrigued by the problems that beset humanity, and you have a sympathetic attitude and tender heart toward them. You see beyond the horizon, and in thought you travel through many lands. Enthusiasm characterizes your services, wherever you render them, and it is accompanied by philosophy and proselytism. You are a good mixer and a keen analyst. In an atmosphere of conflict, you are called on to be the judge and adjudicator. After you have weighed every contingency and estimated the possible outcome, you make the move or pronounce the judgment that you consider equitable. For this reason you have a reputation for fairness that stands you in good stead in establishing your own success.

Second Decan: July 3rd to July 12th Birthdays.
Planetary Ruler: Pluto. Keyword: Method.
Constellation: Ursa Major, or the Big Dipper, representing an assemblage.

A quiet and serious nature distinguishes you. You are systematic in all you do, even in offering your services to those who need them, for you hate waste, and rarely make an overture that does not mean some future return to you. Being of a practical and industrious turn of mind, you know the value of self-discipline. Sometimes you are mistaken for a busy-body; in truth, you are intellectually curious, and love to dissect everybody and everything. However, you do not probe merely for the sake of finding fault; you really want to know. When it suits your purpose, you are diplomatic and discreet. Although it requires some self-control for you to be silent, you win and keep many friends by being a good listener and a competent analyst.

Third Decan: July 13th to July 22nd Birthdays.
Planetary Ruler: Neptune. Keyword: Adaptability.
Constellation: Argo, the heavenly ship.

Quickness of decision, determination, and an ability to fit yourself into altering circumstances are possessions of character which key you to the modern tempo. You are a good talker, and can mimic other people in a jovial and inoffensive manner. A retentive memory makes you a quick learner. Because you are busy with your own affairs and deeply interested in them, you have neither the time nor inclination to interfere in the conduct of the lives of others. You do not generally proffer advice, not because you are selfish, but because of a deeply ingrained belief that people should determine their own course of action. Self-confidence is one of your greatest assets, and you should rely upon it in the varying stream of life.

LEO DECANATES

First Decan: July 23rd to August 2nd Birthdays.

Zodiacal Ruler: Sun. Keyword: Illumination.

Constellation: Hydra, the serpent, representing malefic influence which can be purified only by fire.

Strict conformity to convention does not impede your interest in your own affairs and their advancement. Self-interest aids in furthering your ambition. Fine taste is one of your distinctions. You show this in your liking for beautiful and ornamental things, and you know how to apply decorations to enhance attractions and minimize blemishes. This does not constitute conceit; it is rather like the artist's play with color and shadow. Slow to give your friendship, you are the staunchest friend once you have given it. Your enthusiasm illumines your hopes and your confidence in the future. You have enormous reserves and the capacity to rebuild. What you do, will be well done.

Second Decan: August 3rd to August 13th Birthdays.
Planetary Ruler: Jupiter. Keyword: Intellect.

Constellation: Crater, or the Cup, representing emotional overflowing.

You are a natural brain worker, seeking to accomplish through the operation of intellectual capacities what others try to do by trial and error, or manual means. You are well suited by temperament and choice to lead and direct others. Success has much significance to you, and you particularly enjoy it when you have gained it by means of your own. Authority and responsibility rest easily upon your shoulders. However, detail work bores you, and you avoid it when you can. Sometimes your ambition leads to a slight impulsiveness. Although you are inclined to be quick-tempered, you are easily pacified.

Emotions stir you, but do not have a long lasting effect. Gaiety attracts you, and you can be the life of the party if you choose. Luxury and beauty appeal to you, and you try to have them in your environment as much as possible.

Third Decan: August 14th to August 22nd Birthdays. Planetary Ruler: Mars. Keyword: Experimentation.

Constellation: Corvus, the Raven, destroyer of the enemy.

The alternating currents of your nervous energy produce bursts of speed and periods of relaxation. Routine wearies you and stultifies your efforts. Your mentality requires a continuous flow of fresh stimuli in the form of new ideas, new experiences, and varied experiments. You seek these, and you find them, on the highways and byways of life, making each day a search for the injection of change and variety in your mode of living and of thought. Should you slacken your concentration completely, you would become one of life's rolling stones. The development of one of your many talents might lead to success in some field of sufficient attractiveness to hold your interest. In the complex modern world, you need insurance of some kind to prevent the waste of your many virtues and potentialities.

VIRGO DECANATES

First Decan: August 23rd to September 2nd Birthdays. Planetary Ruler: Mercury. Keyword: Alertness.

Constellation: Coma, the virgin mother suckling the boy infant.

Your mental perspicacity is so keen as to amount almost to prophetic insight. Your aim carries the arrow directly to the mark. Even your words are pointed, achieving their purpose whether it be to inform, relate, or pierce. You like to be helpful for you have a natural sympathy which grows from your understanding. History and philosophy are your favorite subjects, and your vision makes the past a moving pageant to you. A quick wit makes you a person to whom attention is paid, and would make you a good instructor. You are altogether pleasing as a speaker, and you have the happy faculty of achieving results with what you say.

Second Decan: September 3rd to Sept. 13th Birthdays. Planetary Ruler: Saturn. Keyword: Dignity.

Constellation: Centaurus, half man-half beast, symbolizing the dual nature of man.

Because pride distinguishes you, you are impelled to be critical of all which does not measure up to your high standards. You are stubborn in the sense that you will not compromise with halfway measures. Balancing these characteristics is a substantial amount of ability to back up your pretensions and an intellectual appreciation of the arts. In practice, your own gifts run to decoration. A sense of economy enables you to do much with little. On the other hand, you do not pinch pennies when it comes to those you love. To them you show real generosity. An ingratiating nature and social affability brings you a host of friends and admirers.

Third Decan: September 14th to Sept. 22nd Birthdays.
Planetary Ruler: Venus. Keyword: Discrimination.

Constellation: Bootes, the gleaner gathering in the harvest.

An aversion for make-shifts strengthens your character and distinguishes your individuality. It is your destiny to search for knowledge relentlessly and to seek the truth tirelessly. A fearless realism causes you to reduce everything to the lowest common denominator, tearing away the curtain of sham. Your ego and confidence are bolstered by your managerial ability. You need wide fields in which to operate, for limitations on your potentialities make you feel cramped and unhappy. Hindrance or obscurity only impel you to revolt. You draw deep and full from the well of self-assurance.

LIBRA DECANATES

First Decan: September 23rd to October 3rd Birthdays.
Planetary Ruler: Venus. Keyword: Magnetism.

Constellation: Crucis, the cross symbol of atonement.

To you, living up to your greatest potentialities means having a vital personality and the place in life to achieve your desires. Making a good impression on others is important to you, for you take pride in yourself. You seek to gain the good opinion of people you respect through conducting yourself correctly. You are helped in this aim by having as the master planet of your Sun group Venus, ruler of the niceties of life. In normal times and circumstances a happy marriage is your most ardent aspiration. You are good at creating original ideas and efficient systems. You find life exciting because you add your own particular brand of zest to it.

Second Decan: October 4th to October 13th Birthdays.
Planetary Ruler: Uranus. Keyword: Endurance.
Constellation: Lupus, the wolf, slain, and standing for repentance.

Powerful endurance characterizes you, although this force is sometimes disturbed by nervous tension or emotional extremes. Tasks and problems drain your energy temporarily, but you get a "second wind" which sees you through. You are dramatic in your expression, making the small events of daily life very picturesque in the telling. You are a good audience, too, extending the courtesy of listening attentively to everything you are told. When stimulated by the dynamo within or the effect of others from without, you are radiant and magnetic. Nothing peps you up more than an affable crowd in a congenial atmosphere. Your talents find fullest expression in a field where you deal with large numbers of people.

Third Decan: October 14th to October 23rd Birthdays.
Planetary Ruler: Mercury. Keyword: Persistence.
Constellation: Corona Borealis, the crown, symbol of achievement.

An abounding energy makes you seek out the most progressive causes to champion, for these are the ones that stimulate you and match your natural vigor. You function well on your own initiative and act purposefully and energetically without being pushed. Convinced of the worthiness of the cause or reason for your labors, you find no effort too strenuous. Occasionally you give the impression of being belligerent, but you know how to tone down the vitality you apply to the job you are doing. Writing, teaching, or the dramatic arts are successful fields for you.

SCORPIO DECANATES

First Decan: October 24th to November 1st Birthdays.
Planetary Ruler: Pluto. Keyword: Integrity.

Constellation: The Serpent, symbol of spiritual power and occult secrets.

You have a reputation for being thorough and steadfast, patient and determined. Because you pay scrupulous attention to each detail of what you do, you are a trustworthy friend and reliable co-worker. When you put your time or effort into a project, you demand results, and you get them. Your seeking gain is not of the selfish kind, though; it is a desire for equity and an urge to be helpful. You never betray a trust, but you take very bitterly any action you consider a betrayal of your friendship. You adhere to your beliefs at all costs, and would have accepted martyrdom in another age. You have a deep understanding of psychic, emotional, business, and world affairs. You inspire those you love to achieve great heights.

Second Decan: November 2nd to Nov. 11th Birthdays.
Planetary Ruler: Neptune. Keyword: Loyalty.

Constellation: Cerberus, the three-headed, representing exoteric knowledge.

Fame and prosperity are your aims in life, and you are quite well equipped to win them. You know how to advance your ambitions, and how to make every moment count. Sincere loyalty brings you many advocates and friends while hard work advances your cause. You have a great capacity for giving of yourself, and no sacrifice is too great for you to make in the name of your ideal. You are of a romantic turn of mind, perhaps a little too much so. With you it's all-out-or-nothing for love. A serenity born of wisdom and experience enables you to radiate a wonderfully soothing effect. The formalities of life mean little to you; you understand the everlasting things.

Third Decan: November 12th to Nov. 22nd Birthdays.
Zodiacal Ruler: Moon. Keyword: Righteousness.
Constellation: Hercules, the destroyer of evil.

You are a defender and champion of the cause of right. Your personal character includes every freedom, and you want to share it with the world. When danger threatens to curtail a single privilege in the Magna Carta of humanity, there you are to safeguard it. This constant drive instills self-confidence in those who know you, and the same quality gives you a position of esteem in your group or community. You are very much discouraged at times, feeling that you can never attain your heart's desire. These moods of depression pass when you think of the high aspirations you are working for. It is easy to climb a hill; you have chosen a high mountain, so do not falter on the way.

SAGITTARIUS DECANATES

First Decan: November 23rd to Dec. 1st Birthdays.
Planetary Ruler: Jupiter. Keyword: Honesty.
Constellation: Lyra, the harp, symbol of cosmic music or heavenly harmony.

There are no hidden corners in your character where you might attempt to conceal the truth. You like everything above-board, and that is where you keep it. In your relations with other people, you show a good sense of balance and a disarming truthfulness. Conniving subtleties are alien to your way of doing things, and your open manner is your most attractive trait. Whereas the schemers who populate the world might dislike you or try to use you, the worthwhile people will appreciate your true value. Sympathy, amounting almost to compassion, gives you an insight into the motives of others, and you are very generous in extending a helping hand and encouraging word. To be happy, you must live in an atmosphere of domestic serenity, and you try to establish this primarily by being a good example.

Second Decan: December 2nd to Dec. 11th Birthdays.
Planetary Ruler: Mars. Keyword: Thoroughness.
Constellation: Ara, the figure of revenge disbursing punishment.

Duties and obligations are grist to the mill of your daily life. You get each job done speedily and thoroughly because you know it must be done, and because you have developed efficiency techniques to handle it. For this reason people like you; it has enhanced your reputation for dependability. You do not care to have too many friends, but are content with a select few to whom you are genuinely devoted. Although you occasionally gripe about the number of your responsibilities, you generally find someone to help you with your burden. You are an enlightened individual; don't bury your light under a basket.

Third Decan: December 12th to Dec. 21st Birthdays.
Zodiacal Ruler: Sun. Keyword: Intuition.

Constellation Draco, the dragon, to be vanquished by good.

Gifted with a perspicacious intuition and penetrating psychic sight, your impressions are vividly accurate, and they guide you well. It is only when you are reluctant to go according to your inner dictates that you err. Experience is your best teacher rather than other people, for advice may be undependable, but your own past is never to be questioned. Form, beauty, and ritual hold a distinct attraction for you. You can escape into them from the crudities of economics and strife as other people do into the sleep of poppies. Nevertheless you fulfill your duties whenever responsibility is placed on you. Your cares and troubles, however, you do not share. With your friends you count only the happy hours.

CAPRICORN DECANATES

First Decan: December 22nd to Dec. 31st Birthdays.
Planetary Rulers: Saturn. Keyword: Precision.

Constellation: Sagitta, the celestial arrow destroying the evil in its path.

With force and determination, you live up to your standards of precision. Sincerity and faithfulness make you require exactitude in all things with which you are associated. You make it the criterion of what you do, and you demand it from those who serve or assist you. All this does not make you a martinet, nor does it freeze your emotions. You are rather demonstrative by nature, and you like the display of affection towards you. You resent disappointments and delays, and you must learn the lesson that they are a part of life, for everything cannot always be a bed of roses. The law of compensation never ceases operating, nor is it ever rescinded.

Second Decan: January 1st to January 10th Birthdays.
Planetary Ruler: Venus. Keyword: Fairness.
Constellation: Aquila, the dying eagle, going to its eternal resting place.

Your time is occupied by a search for the best life has to offer. Self-improvement is an ideal which dwells with you ever. Those odd moments wasted by others, you use—to correspond, to study, to think, and to plan. You love travel for its cultural benefits as well as the pleasure and romance to be derived from it. Conscientious about your family affairs, you still enjoy solitude and are happy when you are alone. Sometimes you feel that your hopes and dreams will never be attained. That is because they are often way up in the clouds. You really have much to be grateful for, and you should think of your blessings, rather than your lacks.

Third Decan: January 11th to January 19th Birthdays.
Planetary Ruler: Mercury. Keyword: Sympathy.
Constellation: The Dolphin or leaping fish, symbolizing spiritual development.

You have experienced a spiritual enlightment which stimulates you to spread a gospel of happier living. The awareness that real joy, peace, and harmony come only from within has been your greatest lesson, and you want to teach it to the world because your soul is filled with sympathy. This experience has by no means made you a mere dreamer. You are alert to the requirements of a material environment and you are zealous of taking your proper place therein. You need love and understanding to be really happy, but perhaps you have to learn that much of life is compromise, that the air of high places is rare.

AQUARIUS DECANATES

First Decan: January 20th to January 31st Birthdays.
Planetary Ruler: Uranus. Keyword: Courage.
Constellation: Austrinus, the fish, symbol of fertility.

Obstacles and obstructions that block others are mere challenges to you. You have the determination to see things through, the force to sustain your efforts, and the courage to stick in moments of peril to your cause. Circumstances may be trying enough to give cause for complaint, but never of your own capabilities. Experience has taught you to use your powers for your own gain. In a world of competition, you are fearless. Your family is a source of pride and pleasure to you, yet you can make decisions and plans for yourself and exclude them if necessary. You balance intellectual pleasures and duties in a way that makes your life moderate, rational, and full.

Second Decan: February 1st to February 9th Birthdays
Planetary Ruler: Mercury. Keyword: Frankness.
Constellation: Pegasus, the horse, bearing the bringer of good things.

An open countenance bespeaks the honest self within you. Deception is utterly alien to your nature, and the widest gap exists between you and any form of duplicity. People, as a result, place implicit confidence in your judgment and rectitude. You have and keep many friends, for everyone knows you can be trusted. So sterling is your reputation that your motives are never inquired into, nor are your reasons ever questioned. Your own line of reasoning serves you best. You can depend upon your inner counsel for the guidance each person needs. Your tastes are somewhat changeable, and you get pleasure from the variety life offers as its spice.

Third Decan: February 10th to Feb. 18th Birthdays.
Planetary Ruler: Venus. Keyword: Insight.
Constellation: The Swan, sacred and beautiful bearer of the cross.

If it be true that "genius is an infinite capacity for taking pains," then you have genius. Craftsmanship requiring precision ability is your field by nature. Your capacity for exactitude extends to every area where you function. This means you are exact about time, money, food, and particularly about your dealings with other people. Pride in your attainments spurs you on. Whereas your unique talents can give you security and a moderate income, specializing in a particular field would make you a master in it. You should learn how to relax because you put such a lot of effort and strength into what you do. Learn to share your responsibilities, too.

PISCES DECANATES

First Decan: February 19th to March 1st Birthdays.
Planetary Ruler: Neptune. Keyword: Reliance.

Constellation: The Bridle, indicator of the restrictions of the physical body.

A storage house within you of spiritual consciousness is the source of inspiration and power for your initiative and activity. A guiding instinct leads you to your goal, for the influence of Neptune makes you sentitive to what is wasteful and what is gainful. In the good sense of the word, you are an eliminator; that is, you get rid of ideas which merely clutter the mind, habits which restrict the body, and personalities which interfere with your ambitions. Yet you are neither mean nor selfish. In fact, you are sympathetic and helpful to the deserving. You are sometimes inclined to be egocentrically morbid, but the moods of Pisces soon pass.

Second Decan: March 2nd to March 11th Birthdays.
Zodiacal Ruler: Moon. Keyword: Service.
Constellation: Cepheus, the Monarch, enthroned with one foot resting on the pole star.

You have a vivid imagination, which, if correctly directed, makes you a creator in an artistic field. There is no limit to the pictures, words, scenes, or dramatic climaxes that your mind can conjure up. Set down in the proper form, they would gain you a splendid reputation. Fame, in fact, is one of the desires of your life. In some form, you must appear before the masses to feel content. This may be in the role of politician, writer, lecturer, radio broadcaster, or any other part that brings you into contact with large groups. It is well within the range of reason that you might develop psychic powers to a marked degree and even make psychism your career. Your basic studies and interests are in the fields of philosophy and occultism. You have a noble heritage to take advantage of.

Third Decan: March 12th to March 20th Birthdays.
Planetary Ruler: Pluto. Keyword: Action.

Constellation: Andromeda, the woman freed of her shackles or broken chains.

Understanding and action combine to make you a vital personality. You comprehend the laws of nature, and you operate with them to achieve those ends that you feel are desirable. Your mental life is anything but a series of transitory experiences or disconnected links. You employ the intellectual patterns to make brilliant campaigns in the world of competition. Projects which concern the future particularly fascinate you, and you have long yet rational vision. No dreamer or visionary in the accepted and derided sense, you make your dreams come true. You should be successful in fields of high finance and philanthropy. The money you handle or deal with should have some connection with the general welfare. Much enlightenment can come to you from mystic studies.

Chapter V ────────────────

STARS AND THE SEX SYNDROME

One of the latest fads now bringing in big money to the practitioners is "dating by the stars." Advertisements are run in popular magazines and newspapers for a dating service which provides a companion for the lonely male or female—one who will be compatible because the desired partner has been chosen by a computer which matches the two parties to the "bargain" (if such it is) according to their horoscopes.

The computer can do a good job, as far as any computer can. None has yet been able to feed back anything that has not been fed into it. And no human element can be fed into the machine. So much for its lack of potential.

What is truly significant about this dating process is that it demonstrates vividly one of Nature's oldest demands, that, as the popular song goes, "Man must have his mate." And so must woman!

The poles in Nature create attraction as the magnet exemplifies. Three planets rule sexual attraction. They are Mars, Venus, and Neptune. Sexual repulsion, or the opposite, is ruled by the planets Saturn and Moon. These factors play a very important part in mating, whether it leads to marriage or not. In Astrology, marriage is a contract, just as it is in law, whether a ceremony has been performed to make it legal, or not.

Venus in the First House gives the native a very strong magnetism, and makes the person most attractive to members of the opposite sex as well as charming to members of the same sex. Venus in the Fifth House is symbolic of a romantic nature; in the progressed chart it denotes a cycle of thrilling experiences. Mars, strong in the First or Fifth Houses, will donate an aggressive spirit to the native, making that person a real seeker after love, romance, or spirited adventures along the love route.

On the other hand, the power of the planets Saturn and Moon can bring on a feeling that freedom from one's mate or lover is worth any price. How often has the world titillated to headlines announcing the break-up of a marriage that had been in the headlines at the time of the wedding as a truly great event? Some marriages between celebrities have been followed and reported with more fidelity than world news. From courtship to wedding plans to announcement of the clothes that would be worn to spying on the honeymooners—

all have been grist to the mills of the press. Yet the next headline might announce a sensational divorce being sought by one or both parties to this romantic, remarkable marriage. Why?

The answer is in the horoscopes of those oil millionaires, those movie stars, those members of royal families. Once the planets have started the repulsion, which can be stronger than love, it is worth any price to attain freedom!

All literature, especially love poetry, is filled with references to the Moon and stars, especially the Planet Venus which is the astrological Ruler of romance. This Planet takes its name from the Roman goddess of love and fertility. Her personification, the exquisite statue in the Louvre known all over the world, the Venus of Milo, is one of the most admired pieces of art ever unearthed from the distant past.

All forms of art and culture celebrate the greatest of emotions, love. What earth-shaking acts has man not committed in the name of love? From Biblical times when David was a traitor to his friend to gain his wife Bathsheba to modern times when the King of England gave up his crown "for the woman I love."

Plato, the world's first civilized man, according to most philosophers, divided love into three classifications in his great "Symposium." He referred to the divisions as a dichotomy, or sort of ladder, and simplified human relationships to those between man and woman, woman and woman, and man and man. In those days, when men married to become fathers of the race, as was the ideal of the golden days of Greece, Plato recorded the truth of thought for the times, that the greatest of these loves was that of man for man.

Life, love, and sex are not that simple! There are countless forms of love, many kinds of expression of love, and an infinite number of forms of sexual expression. The horoscope of one person will show the most noble form of love as the native's ideal, while another horoscope will reveal the most perverted desires.

The word *love* itself can be interpreted in many ways, for its meanings vary from sentence to sentence, from one tone of voice to another. The whole concept of semantics and of speech is under the rulership of the Planet Mercury. This Planet was named after the messenger of the gods, the youth who carried all communications, from one to the other of the Olympians. In the zodiacal man, Mercury rules the throat. Thus, the word *love* is itself mecurial, changing in its significance with every use. You will hear people say, "Love that man"... "Boy, do I love corn beef and cabbage"... "She loves to talk on the phone"... "Love, your magic spell is everywhere"... And now the hippies, supposed avant garde philosophers of youth, have adopted one of the oldest words to express their new and universal way of life. Their slogan is LOVE!

Every horoscope contains every planet. Each may be involved in some way in the grand passion according to the aspects formed in the chart at birth and in the progressed chart. When a man says he is crazy about a certain woman, he may very well be. His friends or enemies might refer to him as being a lunatic over that woman. Again, he may very well be, for the word lunatic comes from Luna, the Luminary, Moon. The phases of the Moon have long been recognized as having more than an effect on the tides; the power of the full Moon is so well renowned that the New York City police assign extra men to duty during its reign. The colleges profess to attribute the famous panty-raids to the full Moon!

You, like everyone else, experience variety and change in the manifestation of your love emotions because you are responding to the ever-changing pattern that the Planets form in the heavens. The orbits of each Planet are known; the time they take to make their travels through them are known. Consequently, the cycles of your life can be determined. A study of the cycles of your own life and the lives of mature people whose character you know well will reveal that people do not change, they "only become more so." This means that your innate traits are strengthened by the life experience; that what seems a change in the pattern of your loving is only a maturation of the potential that could have been exposed by a deep analysis of your natal chart! A woman shocked by her husband's so-called latent homosexual nature suddenly revealed in later life could have learned that this was already pre-determined. Likewise, a husband who discovers that his sexy wife turns into a prude and nagging Xantippe, or more of a domineering male type than a female.

The school of thought established by Jung (the student of Freud who surpassed the master and includes the occult in his concepts) recognizes the expression of the influence of the Sun and Moon in the natal chart. The soul of the male is referred to as the *anima,* in Latin a word of the feminine gender, whereas the soul of the female is referred to as the *animus,* in Latin a word of masculine gender.

The Moon is the symbol of the female mate image in the natal chart of the male. The Sun is the symbol of the male mate image in the birth chart of the female. A woman who has the Sun in a male Sign will most likely be aggressive and domineering; she will hunt for a husband—and her ideal would be an equally aggressive type, but male. In such a mating, there would be a meeting of two high-powered sex partners. The woman who has the Sun in a feminine Sign in her chart will seek out, or wait for, a less aggressive type; her ideal would be a moderate man not too sexually impulsive.

The forms of love are as infinite as the countless variations possible as formed by the changes of the patterns in the sky from moment to moment. Is love, then, a matter which can be guided by the stars? The answer is yes, for despite the infinite variety of astrological patterns possible, man's knowledge of the stars is older than any other form of written and recorded form of culture. In nations where Astrology is an official branch of the government, records exist which go back literally for thousands of years.

You learn such facts on the rare occasions when a shah becomes betrothed or married. Another historic occasion showing the antiquity of the science of Astrology was when Mahatma Gandhi was assassinated. Five astrologers predicted this event —contingent on the Mahatma's appearing *in public* at the moment he was shot. Each agreed with the other four. This collusion of conclusions drawn from the horoscopes became a matter of suspicion to the government, which actually thought the astrologers were in on the plot to kill the leader! Yet it shows the accuracy of prediction possible. The conclusions were based on research of ancient horoscopes written upon palm leaves and preserved for thousands of years in the official archives of the Indian government.

It is by this type of scholarly research that marriage contracts are made in India and other countries where the science of the stars is in good repute or even official. The cycles of life regarding one's personal love involvement can be worked out with equal accuracy. Love is truly the all-consuming passion of the human race. This is elementary, for without this grand emotion, this universal expression, there would be no way for nature to achieve its highest purpose: to reproduce and perpetuate itself.

The complexities of love and sex are the affairs of the Fifth and the Twelfth Houses. However, the feelings are so dominant in these areas that all the Houses of the chart and all the planets are involved. Because love and sex are both intertwined and separate, because each is the result of such powerful planetary emanations, no single or dictionary definition will do. Nature, if her purpose is to reproduce the forms of life on earth, has used an inducement: pleasure. The sexual act is the most potent experience that the human body can have. The Kinsey report states that sixty-eight nerve centers are stimulated by the orgasm! But there is a duplicity about the act and the pleasure. The pleasure can be had without the actual act of normal cohabitation for the purpose of reproduction. Thus, the outlet may be sought in a countless number of ways. Which one? For the individual? It will depend on his or her individual natal chart and the progressed chart.

Which *ways?* The mother or father may be the object of the fixation. Freud called these the Oedipus and the Electra complexes. The love and sex object may be the individual himself or herself, called Narcissism—and it is a stage of individual evolution not at all unnatural—if it is passed. There is incestuous love and sex, or either or both, between siblings. When an American heiress married the brother of Oscar Wilde she said he had been so sexually corrupted by Oscar that he was completely impotent. The marriage ended because it was never consummated. There is criminal bestiality, masochism, sadism, Don Juanism, nymphomania, morbidity, hostility, and there is spiritual expression. All can be acted out in both love and the sex act.

All will be the outcome of planetary aspects and interaction. In normal heterosexual sex conduct between a man and a woman, the magnetism is plain to see and is based upon the Sun and Moon counterparts in addition to the Venus influence. In other manifestations, where there is an imbalance or abnormality, it may be predicated upon primary aspects, such as conjunction, opposition, sextile, square, and trine. The behavior of any individual may be suppressed, frustrated, mild, neurotic, or controlled—different and varying at different and varying times, according to his response to the vibratory interaction of the Planets and the patterns they form in his personal chart.

The aspects formed between the Planets Venus and Saturn have a very prominent part in the relationships between individuals and on any single individual. The angles formed by these heavenly bodies will control the intensity and duration of sexual attraction. They will influence family, parental, and conjugal relations. They will be manifest in extreme desire, and will govern "the end of the affair."

The great Mahatma Gandhi was married in India before he reached his teens. This is the land where Astrology is officially recognized and marriages are arranged by families, and usually upon consultation with the astrologers. The marriage was consummated on the first night. Asked whether he had been told what to do, Gandhi answered, "No. I knew. I remembered from a previous incarnation." There was issue from this marriage. Gandhi went abroad to England to study, then to Africa to practice law. He became a dabbler and experimenter with "forbidden" things: alcohol and others. Then came his spiritual illumination. This was his first step on the path to becoming the "Great Soul" and the liberator of four hundred million of his people from English rule. With his illumination came a decision: to abstain from sexual intercourse.

Here is an example of the great power of the Planet Saturn, the celestial taskmaster, the heavenly time-keeper, and the preceptor of the moral code. Saturn is also the astrological ruler of the legal code. And the law in almost every land prohibits all sexual conduct except that of a normal nature between husband and wife! The Kinsey report claims that if the violators of the laws against sexual deviations, even between married couples in the United States, were carried out, and the violators prosecuted, over 90% of the population would be in jail!

There are two sides to the abstinence story, as every Planet including Saturn, has two influences: positive and negative. The individual whose sexual expression takes the form of aberration does not consider it abnormal or, as the legal codes describe it, unnatural. To him or her, everything he does is part of his nature, and is therefore natural. To the followers of Sigmund Freud, abstinence provides energy which can be used for great creative works, and is therefore a most valuable and profitable way of life. The Freudians call this type of response to the Saturn influence sublimation. A school of psychology, on the other hand, considers abstinence as harmful both physically and spiritually, claiming that it has a malefic effect on the sexual organs, the psyche, and the individual's standing in his community.

Is abstinence the cure for perversion? Saturn, in its roles of keeper of the moral and legal codes, keeps score. In more than any other form of immediate karma, the price one pays for a life of sexual aberration comes highest. The most liberal of legal codes was first brought into being in post World War I Germany, followed by liberalization of the laws contra homosexuality in France, the North European countries, and Austria. Private acts between consulting adults were no longer against the law. This type of code was re-established after World War II, and a movement is afoot to liberalize these laws in the United States. But, what of the punishments to the individual resulting from compulsive conduct resultant from potent astrological forces? He or she may suffer from unhappiness, depression, guilt, social ostracism, fears, disadvantages to employment, religious morbidity, and frequently, alcoholism and drug addiction.

There are perceptible and invisible manifestations in the variety of love and sex attraction. Uranus predominance in the chart in aspects formed to the Sun-Moon-Venus complex causes one to be in love. In this case, the individual thinks and feels more for the object of his love than of himself.

The power of Mars causes people to fall in love. The kind of action, fast and furious, that this expression suggests is typical of Mars. It is also to be remembered that Mars is a hot and fiery Planet, one which can be said to love destruction by the heat of fire and can thus create a literally consuming passion.

The Midsummer's Night Dream is Shakespeare's dream of love. It is a fantasy in which love potions cause absurd, comic, and tragical situations in which animals, masks, and symbols all become involved. It is a perfect and classical example of the inspiration of the Planet Neptune, ruler of fantasy. It is the power of Neptune which causes one to fall in love at first sight, for it is so grand an illusion that the beloved is perfect in the eyes of the beholder.

Appearance, however, is not illusion; it is reality. It counts very much in creating sexual attraction. Many expressions that have become common parlance are attributable to the influence of the planets. To say of a man that he behaves like a ram is to attribute his sexual propensities to Mars, planetary ruler of Aries, symbolized by the Ram. When one says of a woman that she looks as beautiful as a bride, one is giving Venus, the ruler of Taurus, credit. To call someone two-faced is to characterize him as bearing the traits of the astrological twins, Gemini.

When you say a person is a real home-body, you are calling on the Moon's influence, ruler of the Sign Cancer. Anyone who is always on-stage, has glamor, seemingly eternal youth, has the traits of Leo, ruled by the Sun. The men of this Sign are Nature's lions.

An impression of innocence can come from traits endowed by the influence of Virgo, Sign of the Virgin. To say that an individual has a well-balanced sexual outlook is to compliment the Libran quality of balance, the zodiacal scales. Scorpio is the subtle narcissist, more in love with himself or herself than with others as the Scorpion turns in upon itself.

To call a man a stallion or a woman a sport is to be impressed with those qualities that are associated with the individual who is always hunting—for a sex partner; the half-human, half-horse is the symbol of Sagittarius. Of some elderly compulsive characters one says that he is like an old goat. Both old and goat are under the rule of Saturn, which rules age and aging; and the Goat is the symbol of Capricorn. Acquarius is the Water-bearer, symbolized as pouring out the waters of the soul; here is the individual who wants to love, and to give love. Lastly, there is the individual who cannot make up his mind which way to go, and this is the trait of the Piscean type, symbolized by Two Fish, one going upstream, the other down.

Thus, Astrology analyses the sex syndrome. To know all is to understand all.

Chapter VI

THE STAR KEYS TO POWER

HOW EACH PLANET IN YOUR HOROSCOPE ENHANCES YOUR SUCCESS

An interesting facet of the study of modern psychiatry is that when a patient becomes aware of what is bothering him mentally, this awareness becomes the first factor in his cure! The interesting point of this situation is that astrologers have been practicing this eminently sensible theory in an analogous way for centuries past.

The psychiatrist makes a study of his patient's symptoms, investigates his present state of mind or circumstances, and prognosticates how long the condition will last and what changes will occur. The patient's greatest assistance comes from within himself; the self-help that comes from the eradication of ignorance, the help that comes from restored confidence.

This is the practice that was initiated in the early days of Astrology. A client consulted an astrologer who set up a horoscope for the birth and then for the immediate problem or condition. Analysis showed the causes of the condition, gave the client the advantage of knowledge over ignorance, and predicted the outcome or the alternating paths for the client to follow to conquer the condition or to express his greatest power under the circumstances.

If circumstances can be altered or bettered by knowledge, it is folly to remain in ignorance! It is because this statement is recognized as valid that Astrology has had so many followers in the past centuries.

However, many people never come to the fruition of the natal powers within them because they are not aware of their existence!

A wonderful and inspiring example of this type of unexpressed latent power is Grandma Moses. This eminent lady, known throughout the land, was never aware of the fact that she had artistic talent until she was in her late eighties! Yet she has had exhibitions of her work in the most important art galleries in the country; books have been written about her; her works of art have become modern masterpieces.

It was when her fingers became too tortured by rheumatism to continue her knitting, and quilt—making that Grandma Moses thought it would be easy to paint, and so she started on her career as an artist without having taken a single lesson! This is an example of innate latent ability that the Venus position in her chart, and the aspects it formed with other planets would have revealed. Perhaps years of artistic achievement have been lost to American culture.

Is there magic in the horoscope that such amazing things may happen? The answer to this question is an emphatic NO. But, there is magic in the powers and abilities within you that can bring about amazing changes in your life if you will seek to express them.

To understand fully this rather broad statement, you should now recall what a horoscope is. Your horoscope is a reproduction in symbols of the appearance of the sky at the time you were born, at the place you were born. To repeat, the Sun, Moon, and the planets are accurately placed in the chart which is a reproduction of the heavens, and the placement of each of these celestial bodies predetermines your individual talents and abilities as well as your traits of character.

It is vital to understand, also, since your horoscope is a picture of the skies, that every planet is included in it. You therefore have at your command all the power that each of the heavenly bodies can bestow upon you! The Sun, the Moon, Mercury, Venus, Mars, Jupiter, Saturn, Uranus, Neptune, and Pluto are all active in your chart, and each is a Key to Power and success for you.

The individual gifts of each of these orbs is explained in the text which follows. However, while you read this, and you become aware of the gracious gifts that pour from the cornucopia of destiny, you must remember that all these powers are like the power of electricity; they never are active unless the switch is turned on. It is up to you to turn on the switch, meaning, that you must express these powers, not leave them lying fallow!

Grandma Moses is a case in point; you are never too old to begin expressing yourself. You must never let fear or bashfulness deter you. Each planet in your chart is a key to open the door to greater happiness, self-expression, power, and success. Open the Gate!

Your First Key—The Sun

What is the power of the Sun in your horoscope? This is doubtless the most important astrological influence in your life, for without it, there would be no animation.

Your birth itself is dependent upon the Sun, for this great Luminary is the Giver of Life. The rays of the Sun make possible all the physical animation on this planet. Even science does not know how long animal, plant, and human life would survive if the radiations from the Sun were cut off from the planet Earth. It is known, however, that it would be but a very brief time.

Thus, you should be able to see how your individual creative power comes from the Sun. Your individuality, the traits that make you different from everyone else, the entity that is recognized universally as being yours alone—all these things derive from the Sun which made your very birth possible.

Wherever you apply the energy which comes from the Sun, you are expressing your creative powers. The wondrous changes within nature make it possible for you to move, live, breathe, and create. Without sunlight, plants would wither, and all life would cease. Since, in this world, we exist on the energy provided by our consumption of other forms of life, you can realize to what extent you are dependent on the vast motor system which provides the drive that gives you your expression.

The power of the Sun is therefore in everything you do. Some authors have expressed the idea of "living twenty-four hours a day." Has this thought ever occurred to you? You have the greatest dynamo in the universe at your command!

By making a rational division of your day—from day to day—you can increase your output in ever way!

Your Second Key—the Moon

Life must not be stale; if everything were always the same, you would find that you were very bored!

In the largest sense, this expression applies to nature. For in nature, we find an infinite variety of shapes, forms, and colors. Nature uses a wide canvas, and paints a varicolored picture.

Now variety is the result of the radiations from the Moon, which is Earth's only satellite. This orb or Luminary reflects the light of the Sun, and provides additional illumination to the humans dwelling upon Earth.

Of course, everyone is familiar with the important effect of the Moon's magnetism upon the tides, and consequently upon the economic system, such as its influence on the fishing industries, shipping, weather, etc.

However, there are many other indices of the power of the Moon. For instance, the Moon's own placement in your horoscope indicates the changeability in your nature, and to a certain extent at least, it denotes domestic potentialities and physical make-up.

In addition, the Sign in which the Moon is transiting has been an index for daily activities for a long time. For example, "planting by Signs" is an old established custom. Recent experiments have shown the advantage of planting by Signs and following either an almanac or the traditional rules of Astrology.

There is no limit, however, to the activities one should

partake of to gain the most advantage from the Lunar radiations, for every activity in life is under the rulership of a certain Sign, and you can do best when the Moon is in that Sign. Thus, you have the key to your daily activity—the second key to power.

Your Third Key—Mercury

The greatest difference between mankind and the other kingdoms of the universe is that human beings can communicate with each other in a variety of ways other than by overt actions. This great system of communication by writing, talking, and the transfer of thoughts or ideas by invented methods such as telephone, radio, telegraph, teletype, television, etc., is the result of inspirational inventions produced under the stimulation of the planet Mercury which rules communications.

In mythology, Mercury is the wing-footed messenger of the gods. In Astrology, Mercury is the planet which governs the transfer of thoughts and ideas from one person or group to another.

The placement of the planet Mercury in your individual chart has, of course, a great deal to do with the type of thoughts and ideas that you will have to communicate to others. For instance, if your chart has Mercury in Libra, you will probably have latent talents as a novelist or short story writer, for this denotes creative talent along artistic lines concerned with writing. On the other hand, if the placement of Mercury in your chart is in the Fifth House, you would do very well to enter the field of radio or communications, for success would lie in that direction for you.

The daily use of the ephemeris is also a wonderful guide for you, for it indicates the position of fast-moving Mercury, and the aspects this planet forms indicate when it is a good time to write letters, sign papers, and perform any duties connected with writing or talking. Thus, you have a third key to power in your chart—the power of Mercury.

Your Fourth Key—Venus

Although not the largest of the heavenly spheres, there is no doubt that the planet Venus is one of the most inspiring forces—if not the most creatively stimulating one—in the heavens. The planet Venus unleashes the best potentialities in your life and turns them into actualities! The force of love, which is greater than that of any military power in the world, is under the planetary rulership of Venus.

Your love life, which is, subconsciously, the most potent factor in your life, depends upon the position of Venus in your natal chart and, of course, upon the transits which this celestial orb makes in its heavenly rounds. Thus, a "well placed" Venus, with congenial transits, brings luck in love, happiness, success, and emotional experiences that stimulate you.

Your entire creative ability may well depend upon the placement of Venus in your radical chart. If you have Venus in the first House of your chart, it denotes an ability to be creative in a very original way. It shows that you can start fads, styles, fancies, and that you will have a large following no matter what you do. This is but a single example of the possibilities indicated by the placement of Venus.

However, whether you wish to go on the stage, be an artist, lead a happy life as a housewife, or if you wonder why you have culled the reputation of being a Cassanova or a heartbreaker, you can find the explanation in the placement of Venus in your horoscope. Thus, you have a might force at your disposal—all the power of love; the power of Venus!

Your Fifth Key—Mars

The forcefulness, originality, and aggressiveness in your personality, and the energy and drive with which you carry out your activities are "gifts" from the planet Mars. The orb which governs militarism and war, on the negative side of its expression, is the same one, which in its positive expression endows you with the power to do your job, move, act, and perform the necessary functions and tasks of daily life.

You think of Mars as the planet (or god, in mythology) of war. The force expended in any military activity is the most destructive in the world. Can you think of transferring this same power to a creative activity? It is the same concept as using atomic power for running engines instead of for killing and destruction. It is in this manner that you think of the power of Mars! Mars exerts a tremendous, but unleashed and disorganized force. It is like Niagara Falls, which does not know it has tremendous force for running dynamos, engines, electric lights, and so forth. But when the intelligence of man is applied to the leashing of this power, it is put to great creative use. Thus, you have a great force of Nature at your disposal.

For what may you use the power of Mars? First of all, the position of Mars in your individual chart will indicate how you will express your ideas and emotions. You may be domineering and aggressive, or you may be retiring and submissive. These factors depend not only upon the place Mars occupies in your natal chart, but the aspects it forms with other planets and the transits of Mars in its swing around through the Signs of the Zodiac.

Your Sixth Key—Jupiter

Much of the power which Jupiter, in your horoscope, bestows upon you may be understood from its cognomen, the "Greater Fortune." This name indicates the benefic influence of this planet which brings, according to its placement in your chart, the degree of luck which you have potentially within you, and it deals in great part with your career. In its negative aspects, it denotes those cycles of lack of productivity which occur from time to time as adverse aspects are formed with other ones.

If, for example, a person is born with Jupiter in the Tenth House of a chart, in good aspect to the natal Sun, it is an indication of good fortune in the career. If Jupiter opposes the Sun in the radical chart, it indicates that certain obstacles will have to be overcome before success is attained.

Symbolically, you may think of Jupiter as a great cornucopia from which flow the good things of life. What people generally call a lucky break may be said to flow from the wide mouth of this symbol, which pours forth its largess and riches upon the children of destiny—and everyone is destiny's child!

In the transits made by this planet through the Zodiac, you can see the effect of fortune in your own chart. As Jupiter passes through the various Houses of your chart, you will react in varying ways. In your first House, Jupiter will bring originality and initiative; this will denote what may be called a new start in life. Perhaps, what most people like best is the influence of Jupiter in the second House, for in this transit, one seems to go through a cycle of opulence and material success.

Thus, as Jupiter makes his rounds, you have his power at your disposal, probably the greatest force for success in your life.

Your Seventh Key—Saturn

There are times in your life when you feel that you are being stymied at every turn you try to take. Most astrologers agree that these moods, and the actual blocks in your path, are the effect of the radiations from the planet Saturn which is also known as the celestial taskmaster or heavenly policeman.

How true is this concept? As far as we can measure, man learns his lessons when Saturn is forming an important aspect. Does this mean that all beings must forever face a dejected future because Saturn never stops its heavenly rounds nor ever turns off its powerful rays? Not by any means. First of all, many of your abilities depend upon the placement of the planet Saturn in your chart. Your efficiency will depend upon the power of Saturn, for it is this force that gives you the strength to stick to what you are doing—to stick until the job is done!

Neglect of duty brings one to a sad ending; but it is Saturn's lesson to finish what you have been assigned by destiny. Therefore, you will find, on the positive side of the expression of this planet's effect, that when you do your job, and do it well, you will be rewarded!

There are other features of vital importance that are connected with the powerful radiations from Saturn, which is one of the most beautiful heavenly bodies, being surrounded by moons or satellites of its own. Matters dealing with the earth itself, its minerals, its soil, and therefore engineering, mining, oil and real estate are all under the governance of this planet. Its transits deal with these vital matters as well as with life and death itself. You should respect the power of this force which Nature has placed at your disposal.

Your Eighth Key—Uranus

One of the great aphorisms of all time is the saying in Scriptures that "Man does not live by bread alone." This means that the spirit must be fed, too, by meditation, prayer, sympathetic actions, and all that you do for others. The Golden Rule is familiar to everyone; it might be called the key to understanding of the effect of the planet Uranus.

Uranus is a force which radiates stimuli to conduct which benefits others. It is the world reformer, symbolically speaking, for changes which increase man's happiness, which make life better, which brighten the dark corners of the earth. These are the result of the rays emanating from this celestial body.

In your own life, Uranus can make you happy or make you miserable, depending on whether you use its force for good or for negative purposes. It is not easy to understand Uranus, for the force of this planet may make you think you are doing a kindness when you are only interfering in the life of another person! Your impulses to mingle your life with others is the result of Uranian stimulation. Therefore, be very careful in your efforts to make changes in the lives of those with whom you are associated. If, after due consideration, you decide that you are making a real contribution by your conduct, then you are expressing the positive effect of Uranus, and you should go ahead! But if it appears that you are needlessly interfering, then STOP.

Your Ninth Key—Neptune

Unquestionably, one of the greatest forces in the universe today is that of the planet Neptune which is mysterious, patient, fabulous, and magnetic. Like all other things, this body has two sides to its nature, the negative and the positive.

In its positive expression, Neptune is the ruler of the imagination, the giver of inspiration, the force which produces artistic masterpieces which result from the reveries of those idealists and artists who thereafter seek expression in the form of the dreams they dreamed.

Such a potent force must have a potent negative aspect or nature, and that is true of Neptune. For Neptune spells illusion. The opposite side of this coin, figuratively speaking, is one of waste. Merely to dream is to dispel one's energies to no avail. The power of Neptune is creative only when it results in your putting your dreams into a practical form. This form may be the writing of a story or a play; it may be in drawing a picture; it may be in inventing a new appliance, or discovering a new law of nature; but to dream aimlessly is no more than to drift through life without pilot or rudder.

One of the most powerful dispensations of Neptune is the gift of prevision. Your intuitive sense, your psychic powers, and your interest in the occult world stem from the radiations of the planet Neptune. Dependent on the placement of this orb in your horoscope will be your degree of psychism. For example, if Neptune is in the twelfth House, your powers will be great; your perception will be keen.

Nature has provided a "feeler" which is a comfort and a protection; make full use of the key to the future: the planet Neptune.

Your Tenth Key—Pluto

Pluto is the most recently "discovered" planet in the solar system, and it is a force which has been felt but not analyzed until the year 1930. For this reason, Astrology has not had as much time to solve the puzzle of the effect of this body's rays as it has in regard to other forces of the planetary system. Nevertheless, research scholars in the field of Astrology have made available certain information which more than gives us a clue to the force of Pluto.

You should bear in mind that the discovery of atomic power did not come until after the discovery of the planet Pluto, and this probably denotes the force of Pluto as the planet of conversion. The changes in the elements are probably the direct result of the radiations of Pluto. For example, the combination of hydrogen (two parts) oxygen (one part) is known in various forms as a liquid, water; as a solid, ice; as a vapour, steam; and as two individual gases! The conversion from one form to another is indubitably the work of Pluto. Atomic energy, the combination of elements which can destroy the world is change—a change which is attributable to Pluto!

Thus, you can see that in your own life, Pluto will bear a very strong influence. Major changes in your destiny, as well as in your outlook and character, and certainly your circumstances are very likely the result of Pluto's force.

You can, by exertion of the will, change your whole life! Astrology is a study which denotes the influences and forces in your life. Free will is ever yours, and it permits you to use the key to power provided by Pluto and the other heavenly forces. Open the Gates to Power!

Chapter VII

GLAMOR IN YOUR HOROSCOPE

HOW TO DRAW YOUR MAGNETIC TRAITS TO THE SURFACE

Glamor, says the dictionary, is magic or enchantment—magic influence, spell, witchery, and hence alluring and often illusory charm. Glamor, says Hollywood, is an elusive quality which few possess, but which can be the most satisfactory asset in the world, leading those who have it on to fame and fortune. And glamor, says Astrology, is not elusive or illusory at all, and is the birthright of everyone, bestowed impartially according to the position of the Sun in the natal horoscope.

The only thing necessary, then, to be glamorous, is to learn just which particular kind of charm belongs to you by right of birth—and go on from there.

It stands to reason that the glamor of everyone is not, and cannot be alike. Zsa Zsa Gabor, for instance, possesses the kind of charm that particularly comes from her scintillating blond beauty. But on the other hand, Stokowski, with snow-white hair and speaking fingers, who draws such marvelous music from the orchestras he leads, also is glamorous.

The Era of Plush

Lynn Fontanne has glamor—and so has Red Skelton, two people as little alike in looks or their particular brand of laying a "spell" on others as it is possible for two human beings to be.

The late President Kennedy was glamor personified, principally through his speaking voice. Then there was the glamor of beautiful Lillian Russell with her personal charm and kindness. Her magnetic beauty gave glamor to the "era of plush."

Winston Churchill was a glamorous personality, but not for any reasons of great physical charm or attractions. Marlene Dietrich, a grandmother, has a glamor that will be with her when she is a great-grandmother.

The Duke and Duchess of Windsor have taken their place long ago in the roster of the world's great lovers, which gives them their own particular glamor; but far different is Pearl Buck, whose sympathy for those in distress, whose work to aid in making the world a better place to live makes her glamorous.

It is really only a matter of personality, this business of

being glamorous in the eyes of others. And of finding in what line one best can shine.

The elusive quality is the stock in trade of such girls as the Powers models, but the thousands of other girls who daily fill the business offices in a big city like New York are as glamorous in their own way as any models who ever faced a camera. It is not a case of clothes or special hair-dos, either, or of beauty of face or figure—though naturally good grooming and making the best of what is possessed should never be played down. It is a case of putting the best foot forward, from an astrological viewpoint.

Glamor Potentials

Moreover, a young man—or an old one who knows his potentialities—can possess as much glamor as the most beautiful woman in the world, though in an entirely different way.

Glamor may take so many forms. It can be displayed in some by a liveliness of disposition and vivacity that just naturally draws others. Some may be considered the most glamorous of beings because they are so peaceful and easygoing, with a placidity that inspires others to confide in them, certain that their troubles will be soothed, and their desires and aspirations encouraged.

The interesting and witty conversation of someone who may not, in fact, possess an iota of physical charm and beauty, may set that person right in the spotlight of the glamor stage. Some appear born to travel the romance trail, and though it may on occasion be done vicariously, the understanding that can be given to "love's young dream" by the romance-lover invests that person with a high degree of glamor. There is a great deal in the old saying, "All the world loves a lover," for it gives to those who appreciate romance a lasting and different charm.

Personal magnetism in some can be synonymous with personal glamor. In climbing to heights in attaining an ideal, others may wrap about themselves an unmistakable cloak of glamor. It is possible for some to be considered glamorous personalities because they are good cooks, homemakers, and know how to make guests have the time of their lives. That "the way to man's heart is through his stomach" still holds good.

Attributes of Witchery

Patience, and the knowledge that one can be relied upon, and will always use discretion in listening to confidences of others are decidedly attributes of witchery. And when a man or woman can step into a group or even a crowd of people and chase gloom away by his, or her, sheer sociability, there is a man or woman who will receive all the charm plaudits and win, hands down.

Good sportsmanship in any line, or in any field of endeavor, as well as in living life itself, can give its possessor a charm that casts a spell of its own. There will be no need for such a person to use force to attain recognition. It is given gladly.

It would hardly seem possible that plain hard work can make anyone glamorous—but it can and has. If, for instances, that work is creative, and in any sense adds to the joy of living in others, the creator is likely to be considered a delightfully charming person. The work done in itself is glamorous.

Being a good comrade, always willing to "go to bat" for

a friend is another attribute which lends glamor, and if one can thereby add to the success of others, it also adds in proportion to the unselfish one's magic charm. In fact, whenever something nice is done for another it invests a glamor in the "doer" which it might otherwise be difficult to attain, particularly if the person doing the favor should happen to be the type who usually crawls into a comfortable shell and stays there.

Recipe for Charm

Giving freely of friendship, until it becomes known that a man or woman is one who will stick through thick and thin, who is, as the westerners say, "one to ride the river with," is a sure recipe for a charm that will not fade. And if this altruistic impulse should be extended to include the whole world, the person who so devotes a lifetime to the amelioration of suffering or to the betterment of humanity may come to be known as the most glamorous of all personalities.

Kindness to others, gaiety, a real wish to lift spirits in a world that may sometimes seem to be all too drab and dreary—each of these holds a place among the attributes that make for a glamor that is satisfying and lasting.

Just what line an individual should choose if the desire is to be thought a glamorous personality is not a matter of hit or miss, either. The potentialities are set down clearly in an analysis of each individual birth chart. Study the analyses, to find what innate qualities are bestowed, then set about through this knowledge to make the most of the endowments which can cause each and everyone to cast over friends the "spell" of glamor that is so desirable.

ARIES—It is essential that the children of the Ram find, first of all, the true niche which nature intended you to fill. Tender and sympathetic, in spite of the fiery and somewhat impatient natures which the Sign bestows, you also have a keen intuition which can show just what others most need to make happiness complete. It is in giving such happiness—whether at home, in the broad fields of politics, spirituality, or the stage—and in sharing your own joy that you may find your best chance for personal glamor. Aries also is known as the "pioneer Sign," and not for the children of the Ram was written that old bit of advice, "Be not the first by whom the new is tried, nor yet the last to lay the old aside." Try new things, especially new clothes, new fashions. As a leader, glamor may come with the acclaim of being a "best-dressed" woman or man. Aries, as a matter of fact, might have many followers in his or her glamorous train by creating new styles and new ways of doing things. Inspiration, in all matters, which is Aries' own birth gift, can charm a multitude.

TAURUS—Love is the guiding star of Taurus, and there are no braver, more straight-from-the-shoulder people in the world than the sons and daughters of the Bull. It is your mission in life, in many ways, to soothe and comfort, and because of your passionate devotion to your loved ones, it is possible that you will be satisfied completely to be set up on a glamor pedestal and never worry about whether outsiders think you glamorous or not. But for all the serene strength of Taurus, the calm and power, there may come a time when patience is no longer a virtue, then an outburst of temperament could spoil all the reputation for charm that has been built up. A tight rein on temper can avoid that, and an optimistic outlook bring admirers of the Taurus personality. The Taurus-born are great lovers of animals, so time devoted to the welfare of dumb friends may raise the Taurus glamor quotient tremendously. It can be a satisfactory life work and bring acclaim.

GEMINI—With the dual nature of the Gemini-born, there are so many ways in which you may woo glamor that the list seems inexhaustible. Witty as well as graceful, you children of the Twins may become known as glamorous dancers on the stage or screen, known for your eloquence as public speakers, or for the quick repartee you can bandy about at a moment's notice. If this wit is free from malice, it can be so refreshing as to win acclaim. People may come to know anew, and to appreciate the fact that there are no more colorful, vivid, and original personalities than you who were born in the Sign Gemini. The special forte of the Gemini-born, though, probably is to bring enjoyment to others, by the sheer liveliness of the butterfly natures which can banish gloom and set happy feet to dancing. Only, one bit of advice to Gemini-born—don't talk too much!

CANCER—The tender, but strong and highly sensitive nature of Cancer responds to nothing so much as to the call of home, and the chance to devote a lifetime of love to those you adore. The very fact that the Moon-ruled can love so whole-heartedly and bring such happiness to others surrounds you with a glamor which can make others sigh for a like experience. And, loving home as the sons and daughters of the Moon invariably do—you even may become morose when torn asunder from home ties—it is but natural for you to make your home such a haven of peace and joy that you become enshrouded in a veil of charm for the lucky sojourners in your abode. You are by nature rather more wrapped up in yourselves and what immediately concerns your loved ones than in what outsiders think. For you, love of home is a full-time job. But if you should sometimes yearn for praise from outsiders, there is no better way for you to present a picture of charm than to offer freely the hospitality you know so well how to dispense. Or seek a glamorous career in the fields of medicine or nursing, since you children of the Moon can be so soothing.

LEO—You child of the Lion, with your dreaming, sunlight-loving nature, your passionate love of beauty in all its phases, may find in some outward expression of beauty a career which will inevitably bring glamor in its train. The Leo-born think art, live and breathe it, and whether you choose a career of entertaining that will bring mirth and laughter to others, or whether the metier is gripping drama, the charm you bring to it is one that makes other identify the personality with the quality of glamor—make them identical. Applause is the breath of life to Leo, so why not be frank about admitting a desire to be glamorous—and then strain every effort to attain it, though the work it requires may be hard? However, if Leo should not elect a life in the public eye, with the Leo flair for attracting attention, there should be no difficulty in being considered glamorous, if kindness and consideration, all the same things which everybody appreciates, are cultivated. Leo is so joyous, romantic, and full of exuberant life as to be certain to be a magnet and to charm.

VIRGO—Harmony-loving and philosophical, filled to the brim with a delightfully humorous insight and vitality, you children of the Sign of the Virgin have one special quality which will always endear you to others. Invariably you are able to see the silver lining to any cloud. And how that can endear a person to another who may think the earth covered with shadows! Right off, it may be thought of the philosophical son or daughter of Virgo, "Why, there is the most charming, delightful person I have ever known!" Glamor will have surrounded Virgo, and likely for keeps, since you Virgo-born are not apt to show a depressed nature to spoil the glamorizing effect. The chief charm of rather timid, retiring Virgo—in spite of the capacity of the Sign's children to shoot most unexpected shafts of scintillant wit—is your ability to make others think that nothing is of such great interest as what most nearly concerns the conversationalist of the moment. You can, in fact, say not a word and still be considered glamorous. For you are a good listener, and being sweetly sympathetic and spiritual-minded, are not liable to flaunt an extra keen intelligence in the face of the less well endowed. You also may surround yourself with a wonderful glamor because of your exquisite tastes.

LIBRA—The deep insight possessed by you, as a child of the Scales, into the real meaning of life can be of tremendous worth in a world that too often is filled with strife. In a way, it may be your mission to settle differences between contending individuals, or even nations. You are, therefore, among the world's leaders, because of an inborn sense of right and justice. Great generals, as well as great judges and philanthropists, belong to the Libra dynasty. It goes without saying, therefore, that glamor quite naturally goes hand in hand with Libra accomplishment. To hold this, it is necessary for you to keep it a deep dark secret should you be disappointed in humanity, mourning that most mortals do not know the meaning of fair play or ideals. In such a case, the Libra glamor can be enhanced if the sparkling humor which is a birth gift is brought into play In another direction, Libra's love of beauty is so deep that there never need be any fear that glamor may not settle on your shoulders if a career in some artistic line is undertaken. The beautiful homes of the Libra-born make a glamorous setting for a glamorous personality.

SCORPIO—Strength of character and firm purpose which will brook no turning aside, and a courage to carry through to the end are the outstanding qualities of your nature. Rarely is any rivalry strong enough to defeat you. And since the strong, and the winner in any of life's endeavors always win appreciation also, it is plain that you put yourself in line for being glamorous by merely following the course for which Nature intended you. There is a chance, though, that you may sometimes be too determined. Then you may defeat your own purpose if you become intolerant, even hostile to other strivers in the field of accomplishment. Appreciation is far more likely to come to you if what others do is applauded, than if any effort to belittle is made. Surely there is glory enough for all, and with your cosmic heritage of strength and courage, there is no need to be resentful because others acquire some glamor. Scorpio cannot harvest it all. If you desire true glamor, there is no better way to acquire it than by sharing the knowledge that has been gained, by undertaking a career to teach right thinking and right living. Fascinating, sparkling, vital, whimsical, radiant and slyly humorous Scorpio radiates charm without making a struggle when your natural attributes are allowed full sway.

SAGITTARIUS—The Sign of the Archer has been called the "golden harvest Sign"—the Sign of brave men and women. And truly the members of no other Sign are more courageous in the face of danger, which invests you with a glamor that is ever the merit of bravery. Added to that, Sagittarius is thoughtful and intuitive, ever ready to recognize the need in others and fly to the aid of a troubled heart and mind with the magnanimous gesture which is your characteristic. And although you may be dauntless in facing life's battles, and firmly independent, you are far too generous to take the offensive and start things which might cause troubled moments. Sagittarius wants the world to be happy and, knowing how sarcastic remarks can hurt, you lean over backwards in an effort to avoid making them or approving of them in others. "Deeds, not words," is the slogan of the Sagittarius-born, and you endear yourself to others by living up to it, protecting the weak, standing unswervingly by to see that right and justice triumph over ills. If there is any one drawback that could subtract from Sagittarian glamor that comes unsolicited, it is that you are so impatient to get the world's work done that everyone else around is worn out. Loving freedom as Sagittarians do, the glamor heights may be assured by their own efforts.

CAPRICORN—To those who are dazzled by wealth, high estate, and the ability to wave a scepter graciously, your Capricorn personality may particularly appeal. For if an election should be held on the subject, Capricorn children would undoubtedly be voted those most likely to succeed in attaining those desired ends. Brave, self-reliant, glorying in a struggle which winning means overcoming former failures and going on with indomitable courage to the goal that has been set, you deserve the praise that attends success—and the glamor that surrounds it. Capricornians, moreover, take it so much for granted that you will be looked up to, that rarely do you lose your head when your efforts are crowned with the success you have never questioned for a moment would be yours. Capricorn is eminently fitted for a pedestal, and accepts as a cosmic heritage the right to stand just a little above ordinary mortals. Which also gives an exclusiveness, another attribute to glamorize you. However, it is not alone in attaining material success that you shine. Among the most charitable of all people, you gain gratitude and deep appreciation through your efforts to help others less fortunate. Make no attempt, though, to boss those who are aided. That might result only in lessening the glamor which always surrounds the philanthropist. Be kind, but be patient, also, for you may sometimes be inclined to be intolerant.

AQUARIUS—Aquarians are the great humanitarians, the world's altruists, so liberal and idealistic that you gladly give your substance, to lift others to the heights the sons and daughters of the Water Bearer so plainly see. The only difficulty is that you may become so absorbed in solving world-wide problems that you may need cosmic glasses to be able to see what is going on around you right at home. Vast dreams of human betterment hold you in a tenacious grip. No glamor surrounds anyone who is thinking only of himself or herself. It also may pass by men and women who are living and dreaming in the future to such an extent that they do not make the best of their personalities as they go along. Since the Water Bearer is considered a "modern" Sign, you are fitted to exploit the new, in anything from personal clothing to the latest labor-saving devices, and by doing that, acclaim will naturally come, and glamor follow. Hosts of the world's most brilliant musicians, writers and uplifters have been Aquarians, of whom the immortal Lincoln was one. A career along those lines, anything that has to do with the theatre, medicine, nursing or science—humanitarian work—can bring your life the glamor destined for you.

PISCES—Glamor that envelopes the children of the Fish is yours from birth. How else could it be when Pisceans make their entry into this so-called "Vale of Tears" with the belief that life is not so hard on tear glands at all? Instead, you have a deep and abiding faith in your fellowmen, the quality of mercy that is yours can be generous and loyal and not lose faith in friendship even when sorely tried, and you are instinctively able to sort out the worthwhile from the less desirable, and also have the strength of mind to stick to your tenets under any circumstances. There is a basketful of birth gifts that could not be improved on if selected to order. There are times, however, when you may lose self-confidence, withdraw into a shell. But though you may feel as if you are better satisfied in the shell, you know better once you climb out of it and share with the world your brilliance and natural gaiety—and consequently rise to heights of charm. Pisces has been called the Sign of philosophers and philanthropists, and the trend toward both may be drawn out when you choose a career in which the Fish children can be close to the earth, watching green things and young animals grow. Then you will make your most unexpected and glamorous expression!

Chapter VIII

YOUR ASTROLOGICAL PARTNER

HOW TO SELECT YOUR MOST COMPATIBLE PARTNER IN MARRIAGE AND BUSINESS

One of the vital elements of success is choosing a congenial partner. You may have been puzzled by brilliant achievements made by seemingly incongruously paired partners. On the other hand, you may have observed brilliant people go down in ignomious defeat. Why?

Some names in history have become synonymous with partnership. This is true of all periods of time and all phases of achievement. From mythological times, we have Remus and Romulus. They were said to have been nurtured by a wolf, and to have become the founders of Rome. Another pair of linked names belonging to twins is Castor and Pollux, symbolic representatives of the Sign Gemini.

In Biblical times, Damon and Pythias were linked in friendship. Their partnership signifies, even today, enduring faithfulness and loyalty.

Many partnerships in the arts have been both creative and romantic. In silent film days, there were Francis X. Bushman and Beverly Bayne, and Mr. and Mrs. Carter de Haven. During the same period the leading Shakespearian players were E. H. Sothern and Julia Marlowe. Many married couples are stars of the stage and screen today; Alfred Lunt and Lynn Fontanne, Elizabeth Taylor and Richard Burton, Paul Newman and Joanne Woodward.

Yet in your own case, you might have failed in trying a partnership. Thoroughly perplexed, you might yet have seen success crown the achievements of people with no more talent than your own.

Astrology offers the key to this riddle, for it can show how the blending of the twelve zodiacal types will work out to advantage or come a cropper. Each Sign has the same number of qualifications as the other, but some are better suited to one kind of activity than to another. In other words, they differ in nature and degree. Some are born to lead, some to follow.

When you consider marriage, a partnership, collaboration, or cooperative venture, let Astrology guide you. Read your own Sign delineation with its advice in the paragraphs which follow. Read the delineation of any other Sign to understand a prospective partner.

ARIES. You who were born in the Sign Aries have original, creative ideas and the power to put them to practical use speedily. The requirements for demonstrating success are yours: courage, ambition, and energy.

You need a partner who understands your impulsiveness and daring, and who will slow you down to a pace that insures you against failure due to taking unnecessary risks. This balance can come to you from a partner born in Taurus, for such a person is inclined to a slow and easy pace, measuring situations, and taking in all details.

A partner born in Pisces would also be advantageous, for that sign makes for thoroughness and completeness. A conservative point of view can be acquired from a partner born in Cancer or Virgo.

TAURUS. A partner born in the Sign Aries should aid you greatly by giving you the necessary zest and push to get going in the right direction—toward success. A person born in the Sign Gemini may bring the required aggressiveness and action to the partnership. Your own contribution is a combination of serenity of mind and cool judgment.

Without the stimulation of one of these two types of partners, you might be contented with a minimum of success although a maximum is available. Don't hesitate about choosing either an Aries or a Gemini partner because you restrain their exuberance sufficiently to bring lasting benefits to them and you.

A partnership between Taurus and Scorpio should be successful, for the ability of the latter is excellent in the direction of guiding others. Perhaps the most fortunate of partnerships for the Taurus born is with a person born in Pisces. The encouragement you receive from a Piscean partner should enable you both to enjoy the fruits of your practical, mechanical, and physical ability which is the birth-gift of the determined natives of Taurus.

GEMINI. You who were born in the Sign Gemini are particularly fortunate in that you might just about pick and choose from any of the twelve Signs and still not go wrong, for you are so versatile yourself that you should have no trouble in adjusting yourself in a combination with anyone.

Your preference might lie in a partnership with a person born in either the Sign Taurus or Cancer rather than the others, however, for you are so progressive that you are eager to leap in and try something new.

You like to plunge ahead while those born in Taurus are the more receptive type; they prefer to move with deliberation. Thus you are opposed types, but create a perfect blend. You act first, then think about it. A Taurus partner would act as a brake, thinking first, and then acting.

To your mutual advantage, a partner born in the Sign Cancer would feel responsibility more greatly than you. You might consider such a partner old-fashioned, but his or her steadying influence would be a great advantage.

You might also look with favor upon the potentialities of a partnership with a person born in Sagittarius or Libra. A Libra partner would stimulate you to go the limit to prove your ability, while one born in the Sign Sagittarius would rein in your tendency to change too often because of your restlessness and impatience for success.

CANCER. The astrological indication of the best chance of success for you who were born in Cancer is to take a partner who was born either in the Sign Capricorn or the Sign Aquarius. Abundant financial reward might also come to you as a result of a tie-up with someone born in the Sign Gemini. Since you like to run a conservative course, you should be able to restrain a Gemini partner from wanting to take too many chances. You could swing the pendulum from the erratic side of a partner who is merely impulsive to the energetic side, with profit to both of you.

Although you prefer tried and true methods, it is sometimes better for you to combine your forces and resources with a Gemini partner who wants to get out on the run. You do not always go ahead if you are content, as you are inclined to be, to sit and wait for success to come along and tag you.

If you're inclined to be lavish, which is typical of the Moon-ruled character, you might also find it advisable to choose a partner born in the Sign Leo, since such people are prudent by nature. Their sense of economy can spare the unnecessary expenditures you would be tempted to make. Such a partner would be a safeguard for the future—a kind of financial insurance policy against unforeseen events.

LEO. As has been indicated in the paragraphs directly above, if you should choose a partner born in the Sign Cancer, the two of you would form a combination fortunate in being characterized by strength, courage, will power, energy, and the ability to conserve all these admirable qualities for a long period of time.

The love nature of the Sun-ruled Leo people is warm and

ardent as the rays of the Sun itself. Consequently, you may not be inclined to devote as much time and effort to business as to romantic interests. A partner who has strength of character, an intelligence as keen as your own, and good insight, would aid you to see the material side of life in a clearer light.

A combination with a person born in the Sign Virgo should prove advantageous, for the cool, calm judgment, and discrimination of the Virgo born would supplement your intellectual qualities, and curb your impetuousness at the same time. This partnership should work out well, for, whereas you are inclined to rush into things pell-mell, the prudence and gift for detailed analysis of a situation would create a worthwhile balance, and the latter you can rely upon your Virgo partner to provide.

If you seek stimulation toward success, you might find it in the choice of a partner born in the Sign Aquarius. Such an association would be both pleasant and profitable, and you would be on a bandwagon with a person splendidly gifted for getting ahead.

VIRGO. You who were born in the Sign Virgo have keen analytical powers as well as remarkable power of observation. No item, regardless of how small it may be, escapes you. In addition, you are characterized by an intellectual curiosity that makes you ask questions until you have obtained and absorbed the information that you seek. For this reason, you would do well to choose a partner born in the Sign Leo, since you can contribute to the combine your gift for detail, and a Leo partner can bring the ability to organize and execute.

A Leo partner might be inclined to be domineering, but since your intellect would indicate the reason for his wish, you would see why this should be so. Minor arguments with a Leo partner would prove stimulants to your progress eventually. It would be just as well, or better, for you to be associated with someone who would pull you out of the rut occasionally.

Although astrological indications do not invalidate the choice of a partner born in the Sign Libra, there is the possibility of conflict which might arise between your gift for thorough-going calculation and your Libra partner's desire to go ahead based upon intuition alone. You would have to guard against having your pride hurt when your Libra partner's "hunches" proved correct—which might happen more frequently than the usual laws of chance dictate.

LIBRA. You can do well with a Virgo partner, for such a person's love of order and powers of discrimination will make that partner willing to abide by your decisions. Your warm-heartedness, kindness, and generosity should also bring out the best in a Scorpio partner. By your very example, your boundless energy, you should stimulate an impulse to meet you on your own ground, and neutralize the Scorpio tendency to laxity.

You should never associate with a partner who would be a deterrent to you. For example, if you had a Pisces partner who couldn't understand your intuition, and wanted to know "why" at every turn, you would only feel more frustrated than if you had a helpful collaborator.

SCORPIO. If you are looking for a partner, the best thing you can do is get one who was born in the Sign Libra—if you can find one who isn't doing quite well alone. In such a combination, there is little chance for mistakes being made, for your own judgment is splendid, and you can rely on the Libra partner to weigh every move before it is made.

There is a possibility that success might evolve from a partnership with a person born in Sagittarius, but it would require lots of compromise on both your parts. If you both work hard for your common interests, the energy and ebullience a Sagittarius partner could bring to a Scorpio-Sagittarius combine might pay you both to make allowances for the possible lack of basic understanding between you.

If the type of activity you plan to carry out requires supervision, then you would do well with a partner born in Capricorn. His or her executive ability would match your own, and his or her business acumen would be a helpful addition.

SAGITTARIUS. You rarely miss your mark when you aim at success, which is indicated by your Sign symbol, the Archer. You have keen instincts, and are such a persuasive talker that you instinctively sway others to your way of thinking.

You should do well with a partner born in the Sign Capricorn, for you are a hard worker and might profit by the Capricorn ability to plan to the best advantage. You should be forewarned, however, that the Capricorn partner might think his contribution of headwork more than matches the work you do with your hands and heart.

A partner born in the Sign Scorpio could be a success with you if you both determine to give and take, but because friction is almost inevitable, you would find this combination more or less of a gamble.

Should the trend of your interests be in the direction of experimenting in technical matters, you should achieve the highest success from an association with a person born in one of the Signs: Leo, Gemini, or Aries, in that order.

CAPRICORN. Your main form of expression is in supervision. If an equitable adjustment can be made, you should have great success with a partner born in Sagittarius. Such people love to plough right into action, and you will probably never find a more willing associate.

One born in the Sign Aquarius would bring geniality and harmony to a combination with you, but while you would move along smoothly and pleasantly, the probability is that you would not make out as well on the receiving end as you would with a Sagittarius partner.

With one born in either the Sign Virgo or Taurus, you might form a partnership that would be gratifying and fairly prosperous.

AQUARIUS. You who were born in the Sign Aquarius can do no better than to seek a partner born in the Sign Capricorn. The Capricorn nature, with its love of system, could be a stabilizer for your restlessness, and bring to focus all of your best powers.

Your second choice would be a partner born in Pisces, for he would give himself to the working out of your ideas, and the results would be profitable to you both.

You should get along well with those born in the Sign Libra, Gemini, and your own Sign, for you would understand each other's urge to be constantly on the go.

PISCES. You who were born in the Sign Pisces need a partner. Your shy, retiring, nature requires bolstering up, and this you find when your activity is being directed by a congenial and stimulating partner.

A partner born in the Sign Aries can provide the necessary stimulus to your advancement. It would doubtless prove far more profitable to have such a relationship than to try to steady or steer the ship of destiny.

Those born in Capricorn also make good associates for you, but they are inclined to be too bossy for your taste. Although you are not necessarily daring, you can still control others.

Chapter IX

THE FRIENDSHIP RING

The words of the poet who once wrote that "marriages are made in heaven" have become such a familiar slogan that it is trite. Applied to friendship, though, it would be more than poetry. It would be sheer truth. For if all the bonds of friendship were made with an eye to the eternal fitness of things, as revealed by Astrology, there might never be any broken ties.

So clearly are the hopes, the desires, the native traits, all emotions of any individual delineated by a study of birth Signs, that there is no need to go astray in choosing a friend who will remain one for a lifetime. Possibly some may believe they know their friends as they know the palms of their hands. Perhaps—and perhaps again, there may be unsuspected qualities in those same friends that would never be understood unless the horoscope were studied with a view to bringing out hidden beauties, desirable qualities—and sometimes, alas! undesirable ones—into the light.

The birth chart alone can give a true picture of those who have been chosen as friends, chosen because of some surface charm that would fade and pass away if tried in the crucible of true loyalty. It is said that the camera does not lie, but that is a fallacy. It may show the subject at the best, or at the worst.

The mood of the subject has so much to do with the case, whether at the time of "filming" the pictured one was sad or gay, joyous or melancholy, friendly or reserved, lively and animated or drab and dull. Only Astrology can give a picture that goes deeper than the surface. In fact, it can show the subject as once the man or woman was, as they are now, and as they may be in the future, all dependent on whether or not they live up to the best potentialities of their birthright.

Choose friends with an eye to what Astrology says of them, according to the Sign which Providence has assigned to each. Know them through their traits, good or faulty, and move through life with the serene confidence that such friends are those with a true soul affinity for you, bringing happiness because their worth has been recognized.

Dependable Aries

If you want a friend who will never turn you down, who will stick through thick and thin when the chips are down, look to Aries! Especially should some emergency arise. Aries can be depended on to march right in and bring all the generosity, good nature, and hard-headed good sense necessary to take over and bring order out of chaos.

Aries will rarely, if ever, balk at any chore to be done or favor asked, once loyalty has been given. Even if the favor should be one that is questionable, Aries will not question. Such people will go to the ends of the earth for a friend, and even hardship can be a joy when borne for friendship's sake.

In some ways, however, such blind loyalty may have its drawbacks. Aries can be stubborn, and can be likely to rush headlong into something that may not work out the best for all concerned—all because once the mind of Aries has been fixed on an objective, no argument can turn such people aside.

Innately impatient of advice and criticism as Aries is, it may be advisable for such friends to try to put a curb on any tendency to sweep well-meant advice aside, in favor of the beloved friend it is the desire to help. For under such circumstances, when an Aries friend can be persuaded to listen to reason, to curb somewhat the love of excitement for its own sake, the resulting friendship takes on new meaning, with Aries expanding to display the wonderful gifts bestowed on the Sign—loving tenderness, a hopeful viewpoint even in adversity, and the quality of making one of the best friends on earth.

Sincere Taurus

Taurus loves life. Taurus likes nothing better than to look on beamingly while others—particularly those selected as close friends—enjoy the gifts of a beneficent Providence. Taurus likewise has the capacity for making friends and keeping them. Since Taurus is ruled by the planet Venus, love of others and a sincere admiration of beauty in all its aspects is second nature to those of this Sign. It is true that love begets love, so Taurus of the loving heart is quite apt to draw others until more friends are in their book of life than mere acquaintances.

Quite likely a Taurus friend will be a person of worth in his or her community, but this is all to the good where friends are concerned. For such a good comrade will hardly accent such pre-eminence for the sake of mere vanity. Rather, it will be used for the good of friends, to help them

Sometimes, however, Taurus can be as stubborn as the Bull which is the Sign's symbol, and at such times might display an outburst of temper entirely at variance with the more usual loving kindness. If the pride is hurt, such people may even grow moody, refusing to listen to reason, so that there might be danger of losing Taurus as a friend unless this can be understood. Handle your Taurus friend with kid gloves when it becomes necessary, and certainly do not find fault, for it often is beyond the sons and daughters of the Bull ever to kiss and make up.

Helpful Gemini

Of all the tireless people in the world, you can stack your Gemini friend up against any of them! Especially in a business way can such a friend prove his or her true worth, for the advice that can be given is of inestimable value, since Gemini never will stop until whatever has been undertaken has been completed to the final detail. But if you must consider the cost, you may have to be a little wary. Gemini goes right along with no idea in mind save the final purpose, and the idea of the money it may cost is a mere bagatelle.

Money never sways Gemini, as a matter of fact, for never does such a friend do a favor with the idea of being paid. In fact, the idea that he or she has been of service to someone held in high estimation is all the payment that ever is wanted, or will be accepted. Say a few kind words about how much the help is appreciated, and that is worth more than gold.

Make a special effort to hold Gemini friends, however, for with the restless nature given those who were born in the Sign of the Twins, too often they drop friends who do not live up to all they demand in entertainment and variety. That is a trait of Gemini, for nothing is more entertaining to such people than to have plenty of things going at the same time, and excitement in them all. Gemini wants to be paid by those not friends, however, and when they do things they possibly may expect far more than the effect actually deserves.

Gemini friends are always amusing, however, no matter what else they may be, and their sociable natures will give an uplift that can be highly entertaining.

Hospitable Cancer

For those who love to be accepted as one of the family in a home made happy because its guiding spirit is devoted to domesticity, choose a Cancer friend every time. You may learn a great deal, also, for in some manner Cancer always seems to be up to the minute in every detail of what news there may be about, and is willing to pass it along whether it be in reference to some world event or the latest amusing story.

Such friends also have a tremendous creative ability, which

they are willing to share, but the chances are if there is any work concerned with putting such ideas as they have into recognizable form that the labor may eventually fall on you. Cancer does like to develop the ideas that come so freely, but does not like to be bored with details.

If there is a fault, it is that Cancer sometimes dwells too much in the past, is too "set in his or her ways," and rebels against giving up the old in favor of the new. They may worry greatly about this, and hold off as long as possible, giving evasive excuses for not keeping up with the procession.

Cancer is also among the most hospitable of all people, but loving good food themselves to such an extent that sometimes it can be a drawback to health. The one idea of repaying any favors that may be done for them is by setting a heavy table and inviting friends to share an elaborate meal. Delicious viands to them seem to be the open sesame to everything that is worthwhile.

But when all is said and done, even if you do have to offer a great deal to make life worth living for your Cancer friend, when you really need sympathy and understanding, Cancer is right there!

Courageous Leo

Never look to Leo if you are searching for a friend who will enjoy the quiet life with you! Leo is too wrapped up in searching for adventure, excitement of any kind, including love affairs, for that. But if Leo does consider falling in with the whims of friends and companions as a good deed for the day, then Leo certainly wants everybody to know it. No hiding a light under a bushel for those who were born in this Sign and to whom was given the courage of convictions as well as courage in the more material matters met with in a lifetime. The courage of a Leo friend can carry another through many a hard battle, but make certain that your praise in acknowledgment of that is not too fulsome, or you are likely to spoil Leo who eats up such fine words.

Vanity is a trait of Leo, but it can be a harmless vanity as well as one which may not sit so well with others. Criticism of this fault will do no good, though, and a little flattery may go a long way to bring out the best in impulsive Leo. Though if too many high and mighty promises are made, it is well to take them with a grain of salt. Leo does not mean to fail to fulfill promises, but these are easily forgotten.

The Leo friend, however, can do a great deal toward helping another to reach the heights, to meet important people who can help in a life career, for Leo is unafraid. The highest placed people in the world can never daunt Leo.

Efficient Virgo

Virgo can be one of the truest friends on earth—and can be an opponent to make almost anyone brash enough to take them on, draw in his or her horns and retire to the seat of the defeated. For there is nothing wishy-washy about Virgo. Those born in the Sign of the Virgin seem instinctively to know exactly what they want to do and how they want to do it—a characteristic which is of tremendous value to a friend to whom such help is given. Through following the advice of a Virgo friend, work can simply seem to fly, and without the slightest diminution in efficiency.

It also is one of the endearing qualities of the Virgo friend that troubles can be taken to him or to her, with the assuredness that after a sincere talk much of the worry will disappear like the mists of the morning. Virgo can go straight to the heart of any problem and come up with a solution that makes care evaporate. This probably is because Virgo is such an essential perfectionist that nothing can suit except an answer that will sweep the board clean for a new start.

Should your Virgo friend come to you for advice and aid, however, handle the situation carefully, for the man or woman may be so cautious as to be chary of advice, and might cause a certain exasperation that would not tend to the best in friendship. It may be that Virgo worries so much that they transmit this to others, and some friends are not staunch enough to stand this for too long a time. The answer to this is not to pay too much attention to the small upsets of Virgo, especially in matters that may have no real importance, or should they show a tendency to be tight in money matters.

Such things are of small importance, after all. The main thing is that when help is needed, Virgo will always be there, and you will not go wrong if you follow their well thought-out advice.

Joyful Libra

Many, many gifts have been bestowed on those who were born in the Sign Libra, with its symbol of the Scales. Among them, for well-balanced Libra, is a keen understanding of the problems of others. Their great hearts urge them to give aid and comfort, they have endurance that seems to have no end, a love of beauty for its own sake, and an influence over people that is amazing. All these traits and more have been given to

Libra, with the result that Libra makes a friend who can have no peer—once the Libra mind is set on that.

Librans do have an outstanding fault, however, and it may not always make for holding friends. For Librans are so certain that their own judgment is best, come what may, that they may be intolerant of others who seek to put in an oar. There is nothing that Libra loves better than being a mediator, but with such a determination to see both sides of a question before offering an opinion that sometimes both parties up to be judged may become indignant or wearied, or believe Libra intolerant. Then Libra, for all the balance in the world, is facing plenty of trouble. For both may turn on the mediator with very unpleasant results.

As a usual thing, though, your Libra friend is so good-natured, so pleasure-loving and with the gift of making others see new delights in the beauty so much admired, that it is difficult to be impatient with Libra for long. For unlike the man in Voltaire's satire, Libra actually believes that "all is for the best in this best of all possible worlds."

When things go wrong and the world looks blue, no one can do any better than to turn to a Libra friend for a freshened viewpoint. The drabness will evaporate like magic.

Dynamic Scorpio

There is no such word as "can't" in Scorpio's bright lexicon. It is a firm belief that anything and everything can be done if only the mind and heart are set on it sufficiently. And in most cases, that is the truth. Your Scorpio friend generally does what he or she has set out to do, and the accomplishment is tip-top since Scorpio brings to it a practical viewpoint, and is intolerant of makeshifts.

Work done, however, Scorpio loves to relax with friends, and a gay time is generally in prospect when such groups foregather. Pleasure well-earned is taken by Scorpio as a right and privilege, something that not only is fully deserved, but something to be remembered, It is always the hope of Scorpio friends that their efforts to please and entertain others will not be forgotten. Appreciation of all they try to do to make life a joy to others is the greatest tonic they ever desire.

However, if you want to keep your Scorpio friend in a happy mood always, be careful about bringing up an argument, for Scorpio will have the last word or die in the attempt. Such little skirmishes have their danger to friendship, also, for Scorpio is hot-headed, and unless repressed will swing into bitterness and recrimination, intolerant of the opinions of others, when what had been started as a mild argument has reached its height.

Cheerful Sagittarius

If that old copy-book motto, "If at first you don't succeed, try, try again," was written with any particular sort of person in mind, it certainly was Sagittarius. For those who were born in the Sign of the Archer are so determined to get ahead in everything they do—which goes for business as well as romance—that even if they should be knocked out of the running repeatedly, they will get right up and start again. And more determined than ever. Sagittarius takes such upsets with a laugh, and as a sort of challenge. It is all an adventure, and perhaps what is still to come can bring more satisfying thrills than what has gone before.

A Sagittarius friend draws love like a magnet, respect also.

For who could be cross with one who is so eternally good-natured and cheerful, who takes bumps, grins, and asks for more? That more than makes up for a certain impatience which is characteristic of Sagittarius, more because of the fiery impulse to "get places" and "become somebody" than for any other reason. Usually acting on spontaneous impulse, which is in general idealistic and charitable to a high degree, Sagittarius can be a true friend to all humanity. The only trouble about rushing in to help at the slightest indication that help is needed, is that the Sagittarius-born are often likely to leap before they look, or in other words, they have too much else on their minds to stop and think things over before they make up their minds about what is the best course to pursue. There is a chance, also, that this may bring about arguments which will get everybody concerned exactly nowhere. Sagittarius is so certain that things cannot go wrong, that the greatly desired eventuality can in their minds be as certain as death and taxes—if their method is followed.

With all of this, though, Sagittarius is a loving, tender friend, one who will stick through thick and thin, especially if love is given in return. No blues around, either, when Sagittarius takes command, for such a friend can stimulate another mind to a point of refreshment that a new start seems a matter of course.

Practical Capricorn

If a friend is desired who can be absolutely counted on to be reliable down to the last and smallest details of any problem, call on Capricorn. Those who were born in the Sign of the Goat are an inquisitive lot in some matters. This is just as well, perhaps, for others who wish to follow Capricorn's advice, since such people will never make up their minds or pass on anything until they know the reason for everything. Capricorn always "wants to know why." But when such people do, they can bring to bear all their talents for organization and executive ability, and bring order out of chaos where less strenuous methods might be useless.

Capricorn, however, may not always be the best friend possible to choose for those who cannot measure up to their own scrupulous standards, or those who are not as physically fit to battle with the world. For the sons and daughters of the Goat are themselves so rugged, in both physique and mentality, as a general rule, that there is a certain intolerance of those who are less blessed. Sometimes, this attitude is even selfishness, especially where romance is concerned, for it is difficult for Capricorn to forgive when another errs through loving too greatly.

Also Capricorn may be so satisfied with existing things that he or she objects strenuously to trying new paths, or novel methods, so you need not expect sympathy from these people if your desire is to branch out in some ultra-modernistic way. As a matter of fact, your Capricorn friend may be so set against such a course that it may be felt a duty to obstruct it in any and every way possible.

But when you get down to brass tacks and want the best advice possible in anything that concerns money or business, no one is better able to say just what to do than one born in the Sign of Capricorn.

Altruistic Aquarius

The Water Bearer is the Sign of friendship—so what could be more natural than that Aquarius should make friends with all kinds and conditions of people? In fact, the heart of Aquarius is large enough to embrace the whole world and to desire the good of all mankind. Those born in Aquarius have always been called the world's greatest altruists, and the wish to help others in any way possible is a trait which begins in early childhood and carries through into what is usually a happy old age. It could scarcely be otherwise in a lifetime which probably is spent more in doing things which will advance the prospects of others than in taking time to feather their own nests.

For this, however, Aquarius, is well-compensated by other birth gifts. It "comes natural" for Aquarians to be good business people, and their practicality usually takes care of the material side of life for them. Should they be careless or indifferent about what the future may bring, however, they may be in a position of working for others with no such intention at all, for those others may "cash in" on the plans that have been put forward by the Aquarian who may believe it too much trouble to work them out for themselves.

On the other hand, Aquarius sometimes may try too hard, and this goes particularly for efforts expended in trying to aid others who do not deserve it, and who are incapable of showing gratitude for sacrifice. Not often is Aquarius quelled by this, however, for there is too much confidence in their natures. Thus the course which has been planned by the stars for them to take is the right and proper one which in time will prove itself. This may be lucky for the Aquarius-born, for after all it is almost an impossibility for them ever to learn from experience. They are as likely as not to make a mistake, and then go serenely on and make it again.

None of this, though, can alter the fact that any man or woman is indeed lucky to have a loyal Aquarian friend. Communion with such a friend can lend much to life and make even routine existence seem delightful and a joy.

Faithful Pisces

Anyone who chooses a Pisces friend as a boon companion can always learn a lot, no matter how well-read he or she may believe in himself or herself. For Pisces lives, breathes, and dreams lore of all kind, more and more of it all the time, with never a let-up in the belief that enough knowledge can be acquired for a lifetime. In fact, there never comes a time when the Pisces-born believes that the end of life is in sight, and that everything else can go by the board. The faith Pisces has in the future, and the good it may bring is not only amazing, but awe inspiring. It serves to keep aspirations high in Pisces and in the friends who are near and dear; it serves to keep home happy and peaceful, with little or none of the bickering that may upset many another household. Pisces loves peace above all things, and will strive to attain it with every means within human power.

For that reason, it may be difficult ever to pick an argument with a Pisces friend, for argument without a specific reason is foreign to their nature. They may enter into them, but only to express the theories that have been formed by study. Through that inherent quality which is one of Pisces' chief birth gifts they are able to see "behind the scenes," and certainly into the heart of man or woman.

Being so mental, it is not surprising that Pisces sometimes is inclined to put things off, and if a promise is made, it may be a long time in being fulfilled—not through inability, but because the Pisces-born are rather impractical, inclined never to do today what can possibly be put off until tomorrow. Friends, under such conditions, may become chiding, but that positively is not the way to handle a Pisces friend. All it may accomplish is to send Pisces into a fit of brooding, with the chance of a misunderstanding that might sever friendship.

Pisces is the friend to heed, for when life is gloomy such people can take men or women out of themselves, and make them live in the land of romance and fantasy. A trip like that can make people more satisfied with conditions as they are, appreciating the bright wisdom of those born in the Sign of the Fish.

Chapter X

THE MAGIC IN COLORS

According to traditional Astrology, there are seven primary groups of faculties, six of which function through the cerebrum, and the seventh through the cerebellum. Each of these faculties is under separate planetary rulership, defined as follows: Saturn symbolizes the devotional faculties; Mercury, the intellectual; Jupiter, the sympathetic; the Sun, the governing faculties: Mars, the selfish; Venus, the tenacious; and the Moon, the instinctual. The magnetic properties of planets are identified with the actions that stem from the cerebellum, that is, the physical body and the purely physical functions. The cerebrum is the source of the mental, emotional, psychic and spiritual faculties which are influenced by the occult rather than the ponderable properties of the planets.

By this process, therefore, it is possible to perceive the Divine Essence in the seven inter-related causative stages of life: i.e., (1) color, (2) sound, (3) the sound vibrations in metals, (4) the physical components of metals, (5) the radiant essence in planets, (6) the consciousness of animals; (7) the process culminates in the ability of human beings to be activated by sight, sound, smell, taste, touch and the intelligent use of these automatic faculties.

Through this involution and evolution, spirit becomes matter, and matter returns to spirit. Recognizing this principle long ago, the ancients decided that there is sound in Nature which is inaudible.

The Hindus also believed in the causative principles. Their theory was that the Supreme Buddha at the creation of human beings caused a rosy light to issue from his right eye. The rays turned into sound and became the essence-intelligence of Padmapani Bodisattva (he whose essence has become intelligence). Then a blue ray of light streamed from the left eye of the deity, becoming incarnate in the two virgins Dolma, who thereupon acquired the power to enlighten human minds.

The Supreme Buddha then called the trio, "Om Mani Padme Hum," "I am the Jewel in the Lotus, and in it I will remain." Hearing this, Padmapani vowed never to cease working until he made humanity feel his power in itself, to save it from the misery of reincarnation. In case he failed to perform this feat within a certain time, he stipulated that his head would split of its own accord into innumerable fragments. Humanity, you know, failed to respond. For this reason, Padmanpani's head was shattered as he had arranged.

Moved with compassion, the Supreme Buddha decreed that the pieces be reformed into ten heads—three white and seven of different colors, impregnated with spiritual, physical, and magical qualities.

The story goes on to relate that the Supreme Deity, which possesses no color and is called the "white glory," emanates the tints of the prism. These emit a corresponding vibration in every department of nature. The multiform crystallizations in the mineral, vegetable, and animal kingdom possess the concentrated and magnetic elements of the prism colors.

The clothes you wear, the jewels you buy, and the food you eat are the products of Nature's color manufacturing process—identified in Astrology with cosmic influence, in mythology with divine intercedence, and in Nature with the Law of Synthesis.

Perhaps the most familiar example of relationship between sound and color is the chameleon. Centuries ago this little lizard was known to the Egyptians who marveled at its power to change color under the slightest irritation or excitement. The chameleon blends with any color in its immediate environment at the moment some disturbing sound is audible or beam of light signals possible danger.

By assuming the tint of its background, the chameleon is undetected—unless of course, there is a deliberate search for it by the animals which use it for food or the humans who want it as a curiosity.

There are countless other methods of transformations in Nature. In fact, the process or continuous creative transmutation of color into sound and sound into physical properties—as already explained.

The laboratory chemist working with atoms and molecules knows this. The synthesis of Nature becomes visible and audible to the delicate instruments science has produced—and to the supersensory perceptions the occultists have always possessed. The Chinese call this imperceptible voice of Nature the "Great Tone," or *Kung*.

Yet this voice of Nature can speak in its own way. Musicians found it in the middle *fa* on the piano keyboard. You hear it distinctly in the roaring of the ocean, in wind-ruffled foliage of the forest, in tempest and in storms, in the cooing voice of an infant, and wherever you listen to the harmonies of sound rather than the dissonance of noise.

In Astrology, the tone *fa* and the color green are symbolized by the planet Saturn. Both the sound and the color are phenomena in basic Nature. In chemistry colors are resolved into positive white or negative black, based on the great polarities which are manifested in Nature. In esoteric psychology, however, green is substituted for black because objects in Nature are but shadows of their entities on the spiritual plane.

The occultists claim that even the most beautiful colors on Earth are dim reflections of the brilliant hues revealed by astral luminosity.

Sound also has these properties, the occultists claim. Whatever happens on the terrestrial plane is said to echo in the higher elements. Even the physicists are now working on tonal formulas which are almost akin to the vibratory principles based on cosmic force.

On the popular side, it is well known that the planet Mars signifies red—a super-active, fiery, belligerent color, and that its sound has a violent pitch like the thunderous blast of an explosion. Instead of transmitting the vital Mars forces into courage and dynamic power, human beings utilize it to create discord, tragedy, and destruction. The collective energies generated by Mars are impersonal, without coherent *intentions* to punish anyone for wrongdoing. The vibrations of this planet as well as other planets obey the Great Law which governs, sustains, and keeps the entire universe in an eternal balance. When the vibrations of the Earth create conditions contrary to the law of the universe, the planets automatically attempt to adjust those errors in compliance with its cosmic edict. That the process often involves tragedy and suffering is due to exaggerated egoism plus abysmal ignorance by mankind. When you irritate a bull with a flag, you take a dangerous risk. Often there is no reason for such bravado. Perhaps you do so just to flaunt your intellectual superiority. If the brute force crushes you—who is to blame? The same is true of chicanery, murder, and war. Why blame the red of Mars—which in reality is merely a danger signal? It is like taking a chance with a modern traffic light—purposed to establish a safety zone. But there are always people who try to beat it by a fraction of a second—resulting in horrible collisions. The red of Mars was put there for a friendly purpose—a silent mentor as is the fiery tint and inaudible sound of the planet itself in the firmament. Disobeying the red flash is the reason for the rendezvous with tragedy.

But red also has a precious value—as for example the garnet and ruby. And the red tomatoes, cherries, berries, beets, etc., are an immense source of necessary food elements. Hunters and others lost in virgin forests have found sustaining nourishment in berries for many meals. Is it not clear then that red in almost every plane is identified with energy?

Blue is ruled by Jupiter. This color is used to create good

will and sympathy. Its vibrations are said to be contiguous with the nervous system and auric envelope of humans which the occultists say is composed of brilliant, astral multi-colored radiations and electrovital magnetism. Consequently, blue offsets discord or irritation. Some hospitals use blue painted walls in rooms where nervous patients are treated.

Blue is also a favorite shade in the apparel of highly intellectual people. The blue sapphire is regarded as a precious jewel, while the bluebell and bluebird are among the great favorites of song and story.

One of the most vivid colors of the spectrum is orange, believed to reflect the qualities and attributes of the Sun, the Giver of Life. The Hindus associated this color with *prana*, or breath; necessary for continuance of human life. Therefore, the color orange was used in connection with certain yoga experiences that require perfect breath control. All orange-colored fruits and vegetables contain important juices and vitamins used extensively in modern diets to promote health as well as to correct systemic deficiencies. The bride wears orange blossoms for success and to symbolize the hoped-for new life within her body.

Violet is a rather delicate tint. It is said to govern intuitive faculties. Seldom is it in harmony with colors that have physical qualities. Violet corresponds to the Moon which the ancients believed to be the parent of the Earth. Be that as it may, the violet ray starts the series of prismatic colors that have extraordinary frangible traits. The modern violet-ray machine may be the answer to the occult law about celestial and terrestrial correspondences. Ancient occultists believed that disease before manifesting itself in the physical body was implanted in the astral form, as were discord and confusion. That is why anyone sensitive to super-perceptions is able to read what is about to happen to the astral body on the astral plane. Apparently the color violet is intended to remain aloof because, with the exception of the dainty violet flower that bears the name of its color, there are really few plants that are tinted with this color. The outer skin of the turnip has a faint tinge of violet, but do you know many other vegetables that are of that shade? The amethyst which is of a light shade of violet is said to be fortunate for anyone seeking favors from those in prominent positions.

The planet Venus rules indigo—the occult color which symbolizes the human soul. Yellow, represented by the planet Mercury, indicates psychic abstractions. When the individual consciousness becomes exalted, the occultists say that a conjunction of indigo and yellow takes place simultaneously. In those whose character is almost of sublime spirituality, this color conjunction is permanent.

Yellow was considered a sacred color—a symbol of selfless devotion to a cause. Its effect is soothing, serene, unemotional. Yellow corn is one of the great staple products of the world, and the cornflowers so abundant in field and meadow are the munificent expression of generous Nature. The resplendent amber jewel, which the occultists claim is beneficial for longevity, possesses a rich yellow pigmentation.

As for indigo, that almost blue-black color, it is almost of shadowy substance. It is used only sparingly by Nature as well as humans, for few indeed are scaled to respond to its vibrancy. The electric-blue sapphire is the gem which suggests this highly individual tint.

So does Nature function using the animate and inanimate to carry out her patterns. To those cognizant of natural laws—

it is clear that there are no gaps in the universe. Everything is made to be used—and nothing goes to waste, not even Time—for that is the most precious element of all in Nature's laboratory to fashion her eternal transmutations.

Chapter XI

THE MAGIC IN MUSIC

As a member of the human race, you are actually a receiving set for sound, yet you need no antenna, battery, tubes, or ground. However, except when you are annoyed by cacaphony and dissonance, you never stop to think of the miracle of vibration that puts you in touch with all of nature and of man.

As a receiving set, you, like everyone else, should tune in on the waves that bring harmony to your soul, enlightenment to your mind, beauty to your ear, and rhythm into your daily program.

Your date of birth identifies you with a specific Sign of the Zodiac. Just as you have individual traits determined by the hour, date, and place of your birth, you have characteristics which you share with those born under the same zodiacal sector. And, as you have an affinity for certain Signs, you have a capacity for the enjoyment of certain music. This capacity may or may not now be developed. It may be expressed in the form of making music or of listening to music. But, whatever your stage of development, it is there—latent, perhaps—within you.

Have you ever asked yourself, as you listened to a piece of music, "What do I hear?" Does it appeal to your emotions? Does it edify your intellect? Does it give you a sense of awe or religious wonder? Do you ever feel, as the popular song title puts it, "Where have I heard that song before?"

If you have been listening to music for many years (and who hasn't?) in church, in school, in theatres, over the radio, on television, you probably answered "yes" to all these questions.

But have you gotten the most out of it? There is a music for you which can give you the "peace that passeth all understanding."

Nature's Sound

Where is this music? Where does it come from? Just what is it? A sound created in nature, by the human voice, or by a musical instrument, falls upon the air as a pebble does into water. From there the pebble creates a ripple, which in turn forms waves, spreading over the surface until they break upon a shore. Electronic waves transmit sounds which are expelled into the ether, and a receiving set in your home selects one which you tune in on.

But what happens to these sound waves? Perhaps they extend into space or eternity as do the light waves of the stars which take millions of light-years before they reach us. This is one of the still unsolved mysteries of physics.

Yet it gives rise to truly fascinating speculation. Might not some receiving set on another planet in 2000 tune in on a broadcast made on earth in 1970 whose etheric waves are still rebounding in space? This theory may not be as impossible as it seems on first reflection, for Astrology, a science long practiced and long honored by mankind, has similar *raisons d'etre*.

To the advanced souls, scholars, and mystics to whom Astrology is no game of forecasting, it is known that there is more than one plane of existence. To the true mystic, such as those of whose existence in India we read of, Astrology is not necessary to see events before they transpire on this plane or to recall them from other planes when they have vanished into what we call the past.

However, ordinary mortals use Astrology to tune in on future events as though the science were a psychic receiving set, which indeed it is.

Vibrations

Now, in human living, the greatest influence is vibration. Even in pre-history the influence of the Moon's rays on tides was known to man. Sun-worshippers recognized the beneficient effects of the Sun's rays long before their vitamin content was known. Planetary rays and their influence were studies thousands of years before the discovery of X-rays, ultra-violet rays, and short waves. Now even the school child is taught that all matter consists of atoms held together by vibratory power. And in the march of science, huge machines are built to destroy even the atom, so that man may analyze the vibrations that keep it together in an infinitisimal and invisible mass.

Yet few have ever stopped to analyze the vibrations set up by a bird calling its mate, or an opera singer singing an aria, or a violinist bowing a Beethoven concerto. Despite the subtle influence upon our lives, we have rarely paused to find out what causes our reaction to song. A few initiates in physics have attempted to represent sound pictorially so we might see it. Radio operators scramble and unscramble voices, words, messages, as they transmit them over the air, under the water, and through steel walls—for no fortress is strong enough to keep a sound wave out.

Technicians have imprisoned sound waves upon wax, gelatin, plastics, even steel. They persist and may be heard centuries after their creators are gone—released for countless repetitions by touch of a needle or a beam from an electric eye.

Strike up the Band

So strike up the band. Play. Sing. You can find hours of peace, contemplation, revelation, and tranquility through an association with music in all its forms.

The instinct to express yourself musically is linked with your birth Sign. Each Sign of the Zodiac has a planetary ruler. Astrology knows the influences of these planets in your life. Around the planets, there are moons invisible to the naked eye, and frequently invisible even to the eye whose surface is magnified by telescopes and their high mirrors. However, we know it of old that the movement of these moons creates sound. For centuries this has been known to astrologers as "the Music of the Spheres." And thus it is that music plays a part in your life.

To paraphrase Shakespeare, "If music be the food of love, tune in."

ARIES. Outstanding Musician: Arturo Toscanini, born March 25. Musical selections for your inspiration: Tchaikowsky, Pathetique symphony; Beethoven, Symphony No. 9; Shastakovich, Seventh Symphony; Verdi, Aida; Puccini, La Boheme; Schubert, All Souls Day; Strauss, Devotion. Also popular songs, The Battle Hymn of the Republic, Begin the Beguine, It's a Beautiful Morning.

TAURUS. Outstanding Musician: Yehudi Menuhin, born April 22. Musical selections for your inspiration: Mendelssohn, Midsummer Night's Dream; Bach, Passion according to St. Matthew; Strauss, A Hero's Life; Verdi, La Traviata; Wagner, Siegfried. Also popular songs, Onward Christian Soldiers, Drink To Me Only With Thine Eyes, Auld Lang Syne, All or Nothing At All, Sunday, Monday and Always.

GEMINI. Outstanding Musician: Dietrich Fischer-Dieskau, born May 28. Musical selections for your inspiration: Bach, Well Tempered Clavichord; Rachmaninoff, Second Piano Concerto; Mozart, Don Giovanni; Wagner, Tristan und Isolde; Wolf-Ferrari, Jewels of the Madonna. Also popular songs: Lead Kingly Light; The Donkey Serenade; Giannina Mia; Summertime; The Surrey With the Fringe on Top.

CANCER. Outstanding Musician: Kirsten Flagstad, born July

12. Musical selections for your inspiration: Grieg, Peer Gynt Suite; Sibelius, Finlandia; Chopin, Allegro Concerto in A; Mozart, The Magic Flute; Thomas, Mignon. Also popular songs: God of Our Fathers; Jeannie With the Light Brown Hair; Stardust; Where or When; You'll Never Know.

LEO. Outstanding Musician: Serge Koussevitzky, born July 26. Musical selections for your inspiration: Mahler, Symphony #1 in D; Brahms, Sonata in C; Smetana, The Bartered Bride; Ravel, L'Heure Espagnol; Rimsky-Korsakov, The Snow Maiden; Schubert, Serenade. Also popular songs: Come All Ye Faithful; A Brown Bird Calling; Song of India; Beautiful Ohio.

VIRGO. Outstanding Musician: Joseph Szigeti, born September 5. Musical selections for your inspiration: Beethoven, Symphony #6; Pastoral; Mahler, Symphony 8, E. flat; Elgar, Pomp and Circumstance; Puccini, Manon Lescaut. Also popular songs: Gershwin, Porgy and Bess; Hymn to the Sun; All The Things You Are; To Celia; Lady of the Evening; A Pretty Girl is Like a Melody.

LIBRA. Outstanding Musician: Vladimir Horowitz, born October 1. Musical selections for your inspiration: Monsigny, Les Aveux Indiscrets; Beethoven, Symphony #3, Eroica; Widor, Symphony Antique; Weber, Der Freischuetz; Verdi, Ernani; Puccini, La Tosca. Also popular songs: The Lord Is My Shepherd; I See Your Face Before Me; Tea For Two; Falling in Love With Love.

SCORPIO. Outstanding Musician: Eugene Ormandy, born November 18. Musical selections for your inspiration: Mendelssohn, Italian Symphony; Chopin, Nocture in D flat minor; Field, Concerto #1; Wagner, Das Rheingold; Meyerbeer, Les Huguenots. Also popular songs: The Lord's Prayer; Where the Bee Sucks; Wanderers, Storm Song; You Made Me Do It; People Will Say We're in Love.

SAGITTARIUS. Outstanding Musician: Joseph Hoffman, born November 28. Musical selections for your inspiration: Strauss, Symphony in D Minor; Coleridge-Taylor, Toussaint L'ouverture; Elgar, Cocaigne; Gluck, Orfeo; Gounod, Faust, Jerusalem; Massanet, Elegie. Also popular songs: Indian Love Call; 'S Wonderful; Pale Hands I Love.

CAPRICORN. Outstanding Musician: Pablo Casals, born December 29. Musical selections for your inspiration: Bach, Viola Concerto in E; Franck, Symphony #1; Tchaikowsky, Symphony #4; Puccini, Madame Butterfly; Debussy, Pelleas et Melisande. Also popular songs: The Hundred; Danny Boy; Macushla; Smoke Gets in Your Eyes; These Foolish Things

AQUARIUS. Outstanding Musician: Jascha Heifetz, born February 2. Musical selections for your inspiration: Haydn, The Surprise Symphony; Tchaikowsky, Piano Concerto in B flat; Verdi, Otello; Wagner, Parsifal; Cherubini, Anacreon. Also popular songs: Abide With Me; My Old Kentucky Home; Ol' Black Joe; The Lost Chord; The Last Time I Saw Paris.

PISCES. Outstanding Musician: Lauritz Melchior, born March

20. Musical selections for your inspiration: Debussy, L'Apres-midi d'un Faune; Kreisler, The Marriage Knot; Rimsky-Korsakov, Le Coq d'Or. Also popular songs: There's a Long, Long Trail; I love Life; Memories; Night and Day; Ah Sweet Mystery of Life.

Chapter XII

YOUR PSYCHIC SELF

The world has no secrets, nothing hidden. Everything is objective to those whose psychic senses are developed and unfolded. Do you want joy, grandeur, beauty, and knowledge added to your life? Then attend to the inclinations of the psychic powers latent within you, and make them give scope to your perceptions.

Psychic sight is not distinct from normal sight. It is simply the evolution and perfection of the latter. Psychic activity is of no more miraculous an order, or of mysterious origin, than the animation of the physical organs of your body. It is, in everyday language, clearness of hearing, seeing and sensing—the realization of truth arrived at through no voluntary process, mental or otherwise.

This realization appears on a sea of emotion and mind in which you swim like a psychic fish, unaware of the thing that suspends you, surrounded by ripples and waves of unimaginable fineness. You are immersed in and penetrated with these seas of sensation all the time, but for lack of positive attention and knowledge the psychic world goes by.

How can your psychic power be recognized and used? First, by being increasingly alert to the intuitional and inspirational instincts that well from your inner self; second, by letting your mind dwell on them and analyze their value and significance. And third, by making a practical application of their revelations for a more successful life.

In this matter of recognizing and using your psychic powers, Astrology is the medium through which they are interpreted and made effective. The Luminaries and the planets each play its part in directing the manifestation and governing the operation of these soul forces. The Moon rules memory identified with the past, present, and future; Pluto makes you alert to psychic signals; Neptune bestows the faculty of mystic vision; Uranus generates psychic vibrations; Saturn times psychic currents; Jupiter directs them; Mars gives courage to deal with the unknown; Mercury exercises authority over psychic sounds and voices; Venus supplies the emotional reactions; and the Sun provides the sum-total revelation.

Study the psychic symbols and the psychic power presentments given in the following portrayals for each Sign group.

ARIES. (*Psychic Symbol: A crystal box in which glitters a red stone.*)

You doubtless are unimpressed with the power of your psychic self, and would deny it completely, so determined are you in your attitude toward life and in your handling of all your affairs. But if you consider the dynamic urge that drives you in everything you undertake, the vision with which you can see things through to their conclusion, and the decisive way in which you act, you will have evidence of a psychic power that is as definite as it is strong.

For these are the manifestations of your supernormal ability, and are the reasons why in your world there is a "place for everything and everything in its place." This applies not only to your mental process, but to your everyday living—the things about you, your relations with other people, and even to the matters of your personal appearance and the way you arrange the papers on your desk. All of this has to do with the "following through" character of your makeup, for which Mars, your planetary ruler, is responsible. It causes you to stick to what you are doing, and strip the doing of everything that is not pertinent to it.

All of this shows, too, that you are not impulsive, but think things out with a strict logic that leads to the core of any question. Hence your tendency to meditate, to let your mind wander high above the clouds while you keep your feet on the ground, and through the influence of Mars absorb the psychic vibrations that give you alertness and vitality. When you begin an undertaking, those about you might think a whirlwind has struck, but it is the "supernormal you" which is taking you on to the goal you have set.

TAURUS.: (*Psychic Symbol: The spinning of golden flax for a loom.*)

Yours is the kind of psychic power that, used to its fullest, can sway the minds and hearts of mankind. In its highest manifestation it combines in perfect balance with the spiritual, which gives Divine direction, and provides the strength that champions righteous causes and wins the support of the multitudes. Thus it is that the Taurus born can be great and inspirational speakers, and many of them have made their voices heard through the ages.

And it is this same psychic power that draws people to you for a recital of their confidential problems, to ask your guidance, your advice, and your assurance. For you have the ability to contact forces not visible but nevertheless present, and this ability makes you a friend and counselor. This fact, too, places a tremendous responsibility on you, because any temptation to not heed the dictates of your psychic self could bring great anxiety and perhaps harm to those who seek your inner judgment.

Search yourself psychically and spiritually to make sure that the counsel you give springs from that well of divine inspiration, otherwise the result of your advice may not be to your happy satisfaction. You can mold the patterns of thought and action of those who rely on your word, and you would not want your handiwork to be a distortion.

By the same token, if you have not made use of the psychic power that is peculiarly your own, and have not served your fellows with it to the extent your Sign indicates, now is the time to measure your capabilities in this respect. The world needs what you have to give for justice and humanity.

GEMINI: (*Psychic Symbol*: *An ancient mariner studying a chart.*)

Every person has a psychic quality, and like everything else, it is more pronounced in some than in others. With you who were born with the Sun in Gemini, this quality shows itself in your reasoning faculties, and since you are ruled by the mental planet Mercury, your reasoning is not only crystal clear, but is on the high intellectual plane of the scholar. Add to this the astrologically revealed faculty of blending the spiritual with the material, and you have a duality of endowments that is characteristically Gemini as it is significant to your personal well-being and your life's work.

Because of your psychic power, you can trace with profound right-thinking the spiritual causes that lead to material effects, and also start from the latter and uncover their cosmic sources. How you do this may not be apparent to you, because you may not be any too conscious of your psychic power, but you can do it, and it is due to this ability that persons of your Sign frequently turn to religion, science, and philosophy as subjects to channel their thinking and arrive at conclusions induced psychically.

There is no wonder that you can be a teacher, even though you are not professionally so in a school room or in the cloistered precincts of a college or university. In your everyday life you can spread knowledge—both the theory and the facts—and you can do it because you have the qualifications whether or not you realize them or employ them. And because of your mental sensitiveness you know how to fit the right word and the right action to any occasion. This is psychic power that can be used for formidable results.

CANCER: (*Psychic Symbol: The mystic depths of the Temple of Isis.*)

If you were told you are clairvoyant, you would probably dismiss the suggestion because it carries a connotation of special ability to foretell the future. But if it was pointed out that you of the Cancer dynasty are essentially strong in supersensory perceptions, you may have noted evidences of this fact. This is natural because Cancer is a Water Sign, ruled by the Moon, which gives you a psychic power of unlimited measure.

Since you may not be too keenly aware of this faculty, it is not unlikely that flashes of thought that appeared fantastic to you were dismissed promptly as figments of the imagination too improbable to entertain. But be alert to these in the future, and when your supersensory instincts exert themselves, hold them for their probable value, and check them for their significance. They may be revelatory to a marked degree.

Why not give your psychic powers a test? Put yourself in the mood to invite the psychic impressions that can come easily to you. Be quiet; meditate. Associate your mental images with people and things, and interpret them in terms of those associations. And also concern yourself with telepathy or thought transference, and you may be surprised at the success you will encounter.

This psychic power that is inherently yours need not be used in any professional way, but it can be a means through which you may arrive at solutions to your life's problems, and make for your personal happiness and prosperity. At the same time, you may be able to use it in a broader way, since your objective viewpoints can take you into the service of many people and activities where your foresight can be of great value.

LEO: (*Psychic Symbol: The Sun seen through scarlet and purple clouds.*)

If you have made note of the many times you have been able to "see into the future," to know things before they happen, and it is safe to say you have, it is because of your psychic strength. You may not have thought of it in this connection, and may have been surprised at your marked prescience, but if you trace this "sixth sense" to your psychic self, it may be the means of opening a wider and longer vista of opportunity and happiness for you.

For the more you draw on your psychic power to enable you to see the "shape of things to come" the more aware you will be of that power and the more prepared will you be to meet the problems of life. Since forewarned is forearmed, you have this fortunate psychic gift, and can put it to use in many practical ways. Whenever you receive an intuitive flash, hold it and analyze it for the message it may carry. It may not convey an insight of momentous importance, but however trivial it may appear, it can well be a guide that will serve you.

This psychic strength with which you are endowed has many other uses to which you can apply it with certain satisfaction. Because you have confidence in yourself and are a consistent champion of justice both for yourself and others, your psychic power will act instinctively and assist you in your good efforts to bring order out of chaos and harmony out of discord. It impels you in your forthright handling of all matters, removes hesitancy and doubt as to what course to pursue. Thus you can be and are a tremendous help to your friends.

VIRGO: (*Psychic Symbol: A drum corps in precision march.*)

You are a thought individualist, strong in your convictions and original in your conceptions. With such zodiacal attributes, plus the influence of your planetary ruler, quicksilver Mercury, you have the ability to project your thinking and to give it to others in the form of needed knowledge. In this important service you give full play to the operation of your psychic self and permit it to determine not only the quantity but the quality of your contribution to the spread of information and truth.

But the strength you have psychically can be used to poor purpose if you do not measure up to the cosmic birthright of your Sign—high principles, tolerance, understanding. So you have the duty of keeping your aims and motives "hitched to a star," and then permitting your psychic self to guide them into channels that take enlightenment to the multitudes—for your Sign rules the masses. This you can do—it is your destiny. As your inner awareness points the way, heed its clear signals, and you will have a fuller, a more efficient and effective life.

This is the design set for you of Virgo birth, as your birthright makes you leaders in thought. You have the light of individual interpretation and judgment, and it is your right to use them not only in transmitting the more profound phases of knowledge, but also in the lesser things that have to do with dress, decoration, and the niceties of living. Remember, too, that when your keen and swift perceptions manifest themselves, they are evidences of your psychic forces at work, actively directing you to greater and more worthwhile service to your friends and all mankind.

LIBRA: (*Psychic Symbol: A nightingale hidden in the dark foliage of an orange tree.*)

You so frequently feel and mentally see the results of the cosmic influences called inspiration that you regard it as something like second nature, and fail to realize its source and understand its significance in terms of your life's mission. As a matter of fact, your "inspiration" is your psychic expression, conveying to you messages, illuminating your vision, giving depth to your comprehensions, and providing a spiritual stimulus for your material expressions. This is why you are able to achieve a balance, a harmony, a rhythm in your relations and bring happiness to others and contentment to yourself.

Since your Sign group is ruled by the emotional planet Venus, it is your nature to give things an idealized form, and to translate into the highest concepts of beauty everything you may do in the realms of music, literature, and art. This you accomplish with a facility that evidences your attunement with astral vibrations. This same facility is yours as you deal with other people, since you have the psychic guidance that causes you to do and say the right thing at the right time. Instinctively you know what is fit and proper.

Not the least of the contributions you of Libra have been slated by destiny to give the world are cheerfulness and encouragement. These have their places, and serve importantly in providing the lift that counterbalances sagging spirits, and restores equilibrium. As you make these contributions, bringing joy and laughter to others and replacing pessimism with high hopes, you can know what your psychic self is giving abundantly of its power to make the world happier. Could anyone do more for the realization of man's greatest search?

SCORPIO: (*Psychic Symbol: A deep forest spotted with fiery orange patches of sunlight.*)

Your psychic self is a strongly developed entity, providing you with an insight and supplying you with an urge that is responsible for your relentless search for knowledge and your constant desire for action. Not the least of your armament when you go forth to find truth is the courage that takes you fearlessly on and that makes it possible for you to be a realist. Because whatever the truth may be, you are ready to handle it with all the vigor, the tenacity, and the determination necessary, whether it hurts or not.

In meeting situations of this kind you act with a marked psychic awareness, and are able to draw on your inner power to such a degree that your most difficult problems seem to melt away under the light thrown by your supersensory perceptions. This is due to the ability, characteristic of your Sign group, that guides you through the maze of obscuring thought straight to the first cause of any perplexity. From that point you get a clear picture of the situation, to which you apply your independent and creative thinking with results that are usually successful.

Your friends may call this exercise of your psychic power "uncanny." But if they have any awareness of their own psychic selves, they will know that you have cosmic guidance of singular activity. Your obligation in being so fortunately endowed is to use that gift without selfish purpose or narrow concept of your duty to others. This does not mean that you are to forget your own requirements, but it does mean that you are too much of a cosmic citizen to permit your psychic power to be used in any way that does not share its treasures with all.

SAGITTARIUS: (*Psychic Symbol: The brim of a golden cup over which hangs a purple vapor.*)

Of all the many purposes to which you of Sagittarius birth loosen the power of your psychic self, none is more emphasized than your dedication to courage and enlightenment. No matter what the obstacles may be, you strive constantly to give these benefits to the world, your effort, whether or not successful to the degree you had planned, being an example of splendid devotion. This is why your championship of any cause or your pronouncement of any principle carries authority. Though all who hear you may not subscribe to your views or follow your leadership, they will pause to listen and to admire.

But as you seek to counteract and replace the baleful influence of fear and ignorance, you have the support of that planetary producer of good and ruler of your Sign, Jupiter. Thus it is that your efforts are suffused with a spiritual quality, and you are able to command attention by the sheer psychic strength of the truths you proclaim. It is ordained that you of Sagittarius shall carry the flame of inspiration that wisdom and knowledge might prevail. Your psychic self provides both the motivation for your high purpose and the compulsion that sees it through.

In your service, you do not dwell in the realm of ancient truths except to establish their verity; rather you project them into the future, and apply them to the needs of a new day. In this way you construct the base that replaces the old foundation and on which is built the modern concept of mutual responsibilities. To whatever extent you are able to follow the influences of your Sign you find high adventure to satisfy your fearless urge, and you will take almost any risk if you see the likelihood of success. Your psychic abundance gives you far-reaching vision.

CAPRICORN: (*Psychic Symbol: A grey owl sitting on a shaded hill covered with myrtle and moss.*)

Spiritual consciousness activates initiative. Since the planet Saturn rules your Sign, you are under an influence that gives you profound as well as strong psychic sensitiveness. As a resident of Capricorn you are fired with self-reliant enterprise. Thus you have a combination of characteristics which, working together, bring to you the realization of things done, and done well. It is not by chance that you conform to the highest standards and the eternal truths, and are so exact and careful about details. These are yours by astrological heritage and psychic endowment.

If your tendency to search for minute facts brings you into conflict with those who would gloss over such fragmentary data, do not let that deter you, for it is your task to bring to light the bits of information that added together can be a sum total of revelation. Whether that result is to serve as a guide for your own life, or is to be used for the multitude, its value is proved, and your accomplishment shown to be a tangible thing. Psychic strength is, indeed, the motive power that both guides and drives your factual explorations.

It is this same strength that gives you that inner realization of things not easily noticeable, and an understanding of those spiritual realities which to many are not apparent to the senses nor obvious to the intelligence. Do you not experience frequently this unaccountable unfolding, this insight into conditions and things even though you may be far removed from the scene? Thus your psychic comprehension reveals, informs, guides and advises you. This is a gift of great importance to your happiness. Its free exercise can be your greatest help.

AQUARIUS: (*Psychic Symbol*: *An eagle's nest with seven fledglings.*)

Your astrological gift is strength of spirit, bestowed by the progressive planet Uranus, ruler of your Sign, and evidenced especially in the force of your psychic awareness. This is strikingly shown in your ability to see and know the truth, to avoid the false, the prejudiced and the biased. And this you do whether you are dealing with facts and reality, or whether you are concerned with those things which involve the sincerity and genuineness of people. Thus your spiritual exactitude exerts itself, and takes you along the high road of eminent purpose.

There is fearlessness and valiancy in the approach to everything you do, and a robust quality to your performance that shows you know what you want and seek it vigorously. That you have made truth your goal is the natural result of your combining a spiritualized conception with ethical realism. You do not accept substitutes for the principles by which you live, nor do you compromise when those principles are endangered basically. This strict adherence to your ideals causes you to be courageous as you advance your ideas and put them into practice.

In all of this you are successful because your psychic power gives you strong intuitive faculties, which, when you use them

to the fullest, serve you well in giving you quick and deep understanding and in guiding you surely to the ends you have set. Similarly are you served by your telepathic powers, which keep you keen and alert and add persuasive strength of great value to your life's fulfillment. Hence, your psychic self is a part of you to be taken seriously and given every latitude for expression.

PISCES: (*Psychic Symbol: A learned patriarch expounding the philosophy of ageless wisdom.*)

Perhaps more than any other Sign, you of Pisces are psychic. This is so because you are governed by the shadow planet Neptune, identified with those things which have to do with the mystic and occult. Moreover, Neptune exercises control over psychic activity and quickens it, thereby giving you an abundance of psychic power as well as the facility to use it well. Therefore, if you have found yourself to be unusually intuitive, and strong in the deep consciousness of things that are and will be, remember that it is due to the priceless heritage natural to your group.

With what clarity this endows your vision, which can be called four-dimentional, so farseeing, so penetrating, so wide it is! This is the reason why, even when you act impulsively, there are no blind spots in your vision; you have the instinctive plain view of what is ahead. Thus you have psychic guidance that, if you do not abuse the faculty, will take you safely through whatever situation you meet. But do not mistake willfulness for your psychic compulsion. Sense deeply the inner urging, keeping it on the right road.

The sensitiveness, the reaction to the beautiful, the exalted thinking of your solar group, pave the way for great accomplishment, and the Pisces born have contributed much of their creative genius to the world's progress. Their strong psychic perceptions have given them qualities of leadership which have attracted those who need the guidance of fore-sighted direction. These things indicate the strength of your psychic gifts, the treasures of your cosmic heritage. You have the nature-given ability to turn them to good account.

Chapter XIII

PETS AND STARS

Just when animals were first adopted by man as pets is not known. The association may have occurred as early as the origin of the human race itself.

The ancestry of both men and animals has stimulated great controversies, for evolution presents a diversity of groups, with humans at the head of the evolutionary stream. Yet there are magnetic vibrations of sympathy that are maintained in the great forces of life and Nature.

Astrology explains through Sign and symbol the different

orders and types of life. The "all-connecting" consciousness is symbolized by planetary aspects which denote the vibrations that harmonize the animal and human kingdoms. There is only one Life, but many lives, parts of a stupendous whole.

The Zodiac, its twelve Signs, and the planets influence animals as well as humans. Events in a person's and an animal's life can be closely interlocked by mutual devotion and ties over a period of years. The stories are legion of dogs that have saved the lives of their owners, and of their faithful attachments.

How often have you decided not to go on a pleasure trip because of the possible neglect to a favorite pet? How tirelessly has Rover watched at your door? Are not nearly all birds the "friends and helpers of the human race?" They keep myriad insects from devouring the fruits and crops needed for human sustenance.

Eight Signs of the Zodiac are symbolized by animals. They are:

>Aries (the Ram)
>Taurus (the Bull)
>Cancer (the Crab)
>Leo (the Lion)
>Scorpio (the Scorpion)
>Sagittarius (the Centaur)
>Capricorn (the Goat)
>Pisces (the Fish)

Gemini, Virgo, Libra and Aquarius are portrayed by human symbols.

The animal assigned to its particular division of the Zodiac is governed by that Sign and its planetary ruler. These symbols do not include many animals, but astrologers, through extensive observation and checking, established the planetary rulership of all species and genera.

Isis, Moon, and Cat

The domestic cat is ruled astrologically by the Moon. The ancient Egyptians identified the Moon with their chief goddess, Isis. They revered the cat because they observed that at night the luminous eye of the cat had the appearance of the light of the Moon. Therefore, Isis, the Moon, and the cat were worshipped simultaneously.

The planets Venus, Saturn, and Neptune also influence the characteristics, qualities, and instincts of cats. Adverse and favorable aspects of these three planets to each other and to the Moon seem to exercise an important power in the life of a cat. The felines born while Venus is occupying a Water Sign are not particularly robust and may frequently be ill, especially during a cycle when the Moon is transiting at an unfavorable angle to Venus and Saturn.

Gaunt, ugly, prowling cats which have a tendency to revert to their natural wild condition are usually born under an adverse Neptune aspect. Generally speaking, there are two types of cats, the short-haired and the long-haired or Persian feline.

Though cats are numerous, little has been done to develop distinct breeds except in the last fifty years. The planetary aspects which affect the finer breeds are usually an adverse Moon-Venus combination to Saturn.

The Popular Pet

The dog is probably the most popular animal companion.

Dogs are classified under the astrological jurisdiction of the planet Mars. Some breeds possess marked attributes or instincts which reveal the influence of other planets. Wolf types of dogs, from the grey huskies of the north country to the smallest specimen of this group, the Pomeranian, are governed by the planet Mars.

Sheep-dogs, mastiffs, and other hounds belong to the Neptunian class. Bull dogs have qualities that indicate relationship with rays from the planet Saturn. Poodles seem to possess attributes of Venus because of their extremely affectionate dispositions.

Since the canine race, in general, is ruled by the planet Mars, it is important to observe the position of this planet at the time of birth or during the life of a dog. Mars afflicted by Neptune or Saturn can affect the health of the dog in a serious way.

Dogs are not subject to many diseases. Rabies or hydrophobia, is the principal ailment. Mysterious in its symptoms and action, the diseases belong astrologically to the planet Neptune. Some authorities believe that the symptoms of rabies in dogs and epilepsy (a Neptunian disease) are almost identical. Adverse aspects of Mars and Neptune can stimulate an attack when the physical condition of the dog contributes to such a possibility.

Even if you do not possess the exact birth date of your dog, there are several aspects when care should be observed regarding the health of your favorite pet. Dog owners should watch carefully for symptoms of rabies.

First indications of the presence of the malady appear in an unusual change of habit or conduct, such as a change of disposition, abnormal thirst or distaste for water, fear, and sudden bad temper.

Enemy of Birds

Birds, as pets, are popular for the aesthetic atmosphere they bring into the home. Domestic fowls, of course, have great economic value. The planet Venus governs swans, peacocks, pigeons, canaries, and lovebirds. Chickens, geese, ducks, and turkeys are ruled by Neptune. Parrots are also assigned to Neptune. Sparrows, wrens, and hummingbirds belong to Mercury.

The planet Mars is the most formidable enemy of birds when in adverse aspect either to the Moon, Neptune, Uranus, Saturn or Mercury. When planetary aspects are formed which are identified with terrestrial cataclysms such as tornadoes, hurricanes, and floods, the planet Mars usually is the primary instigator, resulting perhaps in vast losses of livestock.

The setting of hens should be timed to being at full Moon, or during the ten days following full Moon. Hens are more likely to remain on their nests longer and attend to the protection of their broods more carefully, if the setting of the hen commences during this Lunar period.

The health of caged canaries are subject to weather conditions. Great care should be taken that they be kept out of draughts in winter and given abundant sunshine. Unfavorable aspects created by lunations that involve Neptune, Saturn, Mars or Venus may cause canaries to catch cold or otherwise become sick. This is also true of parrots, which are ruled by Neptune.

Fish and Pisces

Household aquariums are familiar Neptunian items of hobby

and pet lore. Pisces, the twelfth Sign of the Zodiac, is represented by two fish, one going upstream, the other down. All types of fish belong to the Sign of Pisces and its planetary counterpart, Neptune.

In recent years tropical fish have become popular. Stangely enough, the aquarium in the home achieved initial popularity in the years preceding the American Civil War when Neptune was occupying Pisces, the Sign which it rules. Again in the years 1901 to 1916 the parlor fish bowl surrounded by ferns and palms assumed a prominent place in the conservatory bay-window.

This was while Neptune was transiting Cancer, another water Sign. The next cycle brought Neptune into Leo, a fire Sign, ruled by the Sun, during which time the keeping of tropical fish, natives of a hot sunny climate, became a hobby.

Unfavorable aspects of the Moon to Neptune affect fish of all varieties, especially those kept indoors in tanks. Diseases of fish are usually caused by parasites or fungi, common Neptunian enemies. The loss of pet fish is likely to occur when the Moon is in adverse aspect to Neptune. Great care should be taken not to injure these pets when removing them from and replacing them in the aquarium at the time water is changed or the tank cleaned.

Frogs, toads, chameleons, baby alligators, tortoises and turtles are frequently adopted as pets, but not so widely in America as in some European countries. They are all assigned astrologically to the rulership of Neptune.

Love and Fear

Small wild animals which belong to the Neptune group are monkeys, opossums, racoons, and squirrels. Monkeys, suitable as pets, are rare. As they grow older they usually develop vicious and dangerous tempers. Their Neptunian disposition and the inability to determine their astrological aspects make them undesirable companions.

Anyone with adverse Neptune configurations should avoid having monkeys as pets. This also applies to opossums, racoons, and squirrels, though these animals may not inflict injury so much as destroy material possessions.

People who have Mars in adverse aspect to one of the major planets in their personal charts seldom like dogs because they fear them and do not trust them. Mars harmoniously situated in the chart creates great love for members of the canine race.

Persons born with Moon in Cancer, Taurus, and Libra prefer cats for pets, if the Moon is well aspected to the other planets. Those of any Sign of the Zodiac whose natal horoscope shows Neptune in adverse position seldom care for animals at all, but are capable of strong sympathy and affection for birds and fowls.

Contrary to surface astrological symbology, animals such as cats and dogs born in water Signs fear the water, drink little of it, and do not like to be bathed. Persons born in water Signs seldom have fish in the home, showing no particular interest in them. Yet men who have the Moon in the earth Sign Capricorn, which is symbolized by the "Goat," are usually fond of goats, sheep, and rabbits, and may even do well commercially in the raising of these stocks for gain.

All Life Precious

Pisceans have been known to be expert, successful poultry breeders and dealers, especially if Neptune, their planetary ruler, is favorably and strongly aspected. Sagittarians harmonize well with horses, providing it is in the breeding and care of these quadrupeds in which they are interested. Horse racing in its speculative phases does not favor Sagittarians, and they should neither bet nor gamble on running horses.

Good aspects of Venus in your chart, regardless of your birth Sign, may make you a great lover of birds.

Planet vibrations between the animal and human kingdoms are so closely interwoven that those who make a study of the inter-relationship of the two can readily discern the subtle reactions that occurs constantly between them.

Great Nature, in its inner and outer sense, is continuously in touch with thoughts and physical needs of each human. Everyone is born with certain characteristics that have their correspondences in the mineral, vegetable, and animal kingdom. In reality, there is no department of Nature which does not respond to an evolvement of human consciousness.

Swedenborg, the Scandinavian seer, called this a "divine essence" manifested as "love," a universal agent which makes all things fundamentally a pulsating, perfect unity. Therefore all life is cosmic, universal, sacred, and precious.

"Those who kill in wanton destruction and ruthless cruelty reveal traits lower than in savage or beast."

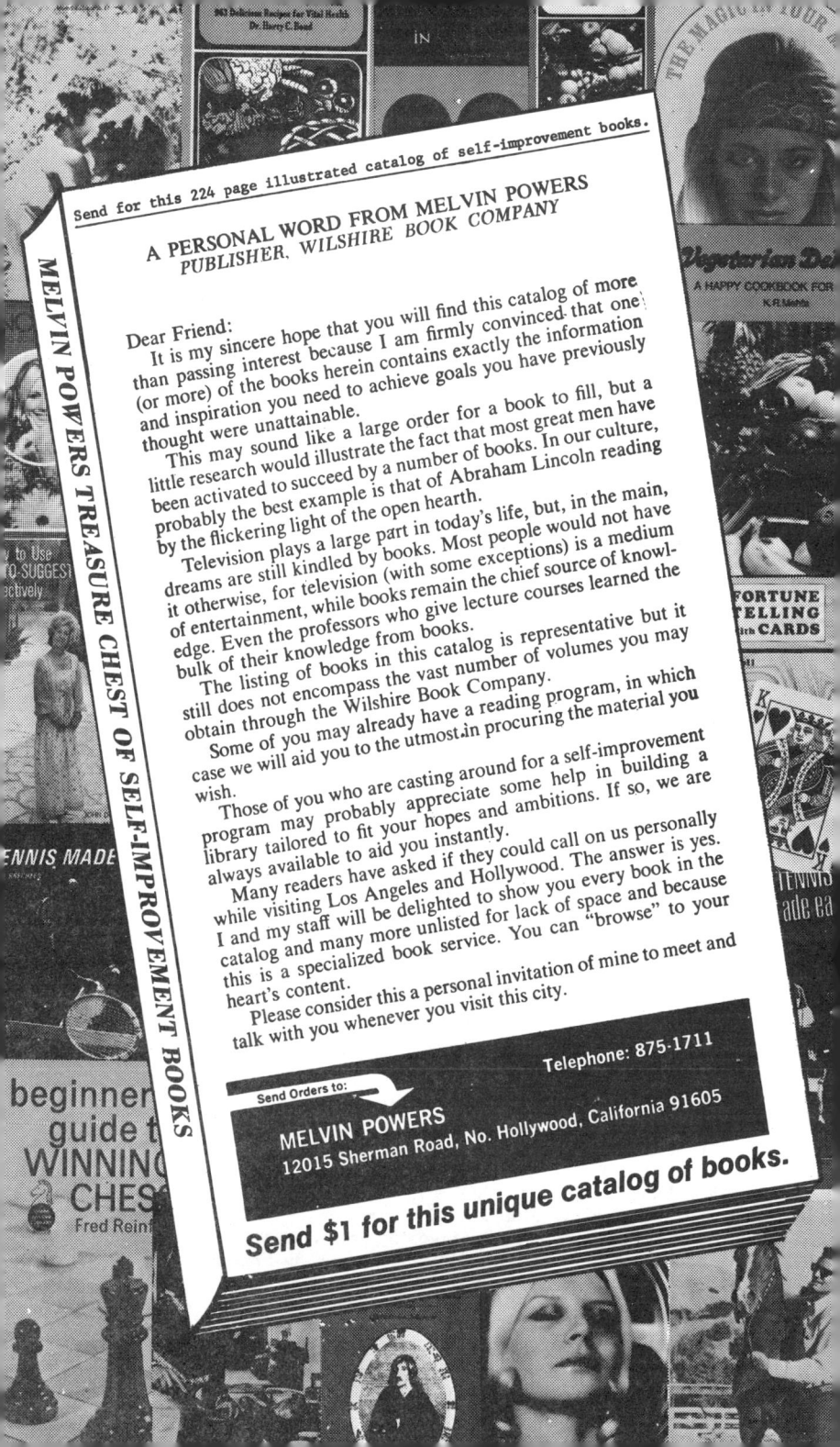

Send for this 224 page illustrated catalog of self-improvement books.

A PERSONAL WORD FROM MELVIN POWERS
PUBLISHER, WILSHIRE BOOK COMPANY

Dear Friend:

It is my sincere hope that you will find this catalog of more than passing interest because I am firmly convinced that one (or more) of the books herein contains exactly the information and inspiration you need to achieve goals you have previously thought were unattainable.

This may sound like a large order for a book to fill, but a little research would illustrate the fact that most great men have been activated to succeed by a number of books. In our culture, probably the best example is that of Abraham Lincoln reading by the flickering light of the open hearth.

Television plays a large part in today's life, but, in the main, dreams are still kindled by books. Most people would not have it otherwise, for television (with some exceptions) is a medium of entertainment, while books remain the chief source of knowledge. Even the professors who give lecture courses learned the bulk of their knowledge from books.

The listing of books in this catalog is representative but it still does not encompass the vast number of volumes you may obtain through the Wilshire Book Company.

Some of you may already have a reading program, in which case we will aid you to the utmost in procuring the material you wish.

Those of you who are casting around for a self-improvement program may probably appreciate some help in building a library tailored to fit your hopes and ambitions. If so, we are always available to aid you instantly.

Many readers have asked if they could call on us personally while visiting Los Angeles and Hollywood. The answer is yes. I and my staff will be delighted to show you every book in the catalog and many more unlisted for lack of space and because this is a specialized book service. You can "browse" to your heart's content.

Please consider this a personal invitation of mine to meet and talk with you whenever you visit this city.

Telephone: 875-1711

Send Orders to:
MELVIN POWERS
12015 Sherman Road, No. Hollywood, California 91605

Send $1 for this unique catalog of books.

Melvin Powers
SELF-IMPROVEMENT LIBRARY

ASTROLOGY

ASTROLOGY: A FASCINATING HISTORY P. Naylor	2.00
ASTROLOGY: HOW TO CHART YOUR HOROSCOPE Max Heindel	2.00
ASTROLOGY: YOUR PERSONAL SUN-SIGN GUIDE Beatrice Ryder	2.00
ASTROLOGY FOR EVERYDAY LIVING Janet Harris	2.00
ASTROLOGY GUIDE TO GOOD HEALTH Alexandra Kayhle	2.00
ASTROLOGY MADE EASY Astarte	2.00
ASTROLOGY MADE PRACTICAL Alexandra Kayhle	2.00
ASTROLOGY, ROMANCE, YOU AND THE STARS Anthony Norvell	3.00
MY WORLD OF ASTROLOGY Sydney Omarr	3.00
THOUGHT DIAL Sydney Omarr	2.00
ZODIAC REVEALED Rupert Gleadow	2.00

BRIDGE & POKER

BRIDGE BIDDING MADE EASY Edwin Kantar	5.00
BRIDGE CONVENTIONS Edwin Kantar	4.00
HOW TO IMPROVE YOUR BRIDGE Alfred Sheinwold	2.00
HOW TO WIN AT POKER Terence Reese & Anthony T. Watkins	2.00

BUSINESS, STUDY & REFERENCE

CONVERSATION MADE EASY Elliot Russell	2.00
EXAM SECRET Dennis B. Jackson	2.00
HOW TO BE A COMEDIAN FOR FUN & PROFIT King & Laufer	2.00
HOW TO DEVELOP A BETTER SPEAKING VOICE M. Hellier	2.00
HOW TO MAKE A FORTUNE IN REAL ESTATE Albert Winnikoff	3.00
HOW TO MAKE MONEY IN REAL ESTATE Stanley L. McMichael	2.00
INCREASE YOUR LEARNING POWER Geoffrey A. Dudley	2.00
MAGIC OF NUMBERS Robert Tocquet	2.00
PRACTICAL GUIDE TO BETTER CONCENTRATION Melvin Powers	2.00
PRACTICAL GUIDE TO PUBLIC SPEAKING Maurice Forley	2.00
7 DAYS TO FASTER READING William S. Schaill	2.00
STUDENT'S GUIDE TO BETTER GRADES J. A. Rickard	2.00
STUDENT'S GUIDE TO EFFICIENT STUDY D. E. James	1.00
TEST YOURSELF – Find Your Hidden Talent Jack Shafer	2.00
YOUR WILL & WHAT TO DO ABOUT IT Attorney Samuel G. Kling	2.00

CHESS & CHECKERS

BEGINNER'S GUIDE TO WINNING CHESS Fred Reinfeld	2.00
BETTER CHESS – How to Play Fred Reinfeld	2.00
CHECKERS MADE EASY Tom Wiswell	2.00
CHESS IN TEN EASY LESSONS Larry Evans	2.00
CHESS MADE EASY Milton L. Hanauer	2.00
CHESS MASTERY – A New Approach Fred Reinfeld	2.00
CHESS PROBLEMS FOR BEGINNERS edited by Fred Reinfeld	2.00
CHESS SECRETS REVEALED Fred Reinfeld	2.00
CHESS STRATEGY – An Expert's Guide Fred Reinfeld	2.00
CHESS TACTICS FOR BEGINNERS edited by Fred Reinfeld	2.00
CHESS THEORY & PRACTICE Morry & Mitchell	2.00
HOW TO WIN AT CHECKERS Fred Reinfeld	2.00
1001 BRILLIANT WAYS TO CHECKMATE Fred Reinfeld	2.00

Melvin Powers
SELF-IMPROVEMENT LIBRARY

____1001 WINNING CHESS SACRIFICES & COMBINATIONS Fred Reinfeld	2.00

COOKERY & HERBS

____CULPEPER'S HERBAL REMEDIES Dr. Nicholas Culpeper	2.00
____FAST GOURMET COOKBOOK Poppy Cannon	2.50
____HEALING POWER OF HERBS May Bethel	2.00
____HERB HANDBOOK Dawn MacLeod	2.00
____HERBS FOR COOKING AND HEALING Dr. Donald Law	2.00
____HERBS FOR HEALTH How to Grow & Use Them Louise Evans Doole	2.00
____HOME GARDEN COOKBOOK Delicious Natural Food Recipes Ken Kraft	3.00
____NATURAL FOOD COOKBOOK Dr. Harry C. Bond	2.00
____NATURE'S MEDICINES Richard Lucas	2.00
____VEGETABLE GARDENING FOR BEGINNERS Hugh Wiberg	2.00
____VEGETABLES FOR TODAY'S GARDENS R. Milton Carleton	2.00
____VEGETARIAN COOKERY Janet Walker	2.00
____VEGETARIAN COOKING MADE EASY & DELECTABLE Veronica Vezza	2.00
____VEGETARIAN DELIGHTS – A Happy Cookbook for Health K. R. Mehta	2.00
____VEGETARIAN GOURMET COOKBOOK Joyce McKinnel	2.00

HEALTH

____DR. LINDNER'S SPECIAL WEIGHT CONTROL METHOD	1.00
____GAYELORD HAUSER'S NEW GUIDE TO INTELLIGENT REDUCING	3.00
____HELP YOURSELF TO BETTER SIGHT Margaret Darst Corbett	2.00
____HOW TO IMPROVE YOUR VISION Dr. Robert A. Kraskin	2.00
____HOW TO SLEEP WITHOUT PILLS Dr. David F. Tracy	1.00
____HOW YOU CAN STOP SMOKING PERMANENTLY Ernest Caldwell	2.00
____LSD – THE AGE OF MIND Bernard Roseman	2.00
____MIND OVER PLATTER Peter G. Lindner, M.D.	2.00
____NEW CARBOHYDRATE DIET COUNTER Patti Lopez-Pereira	1.00
____PEYOTE STORY Bernard Roseman	2.00
____PSYCHEDELIC ECSTASY William Marshall & Gilbert W. Taylor	2.00
____YOU CAN LEARN TO RELAX Dr. Samuel Gutwirth	2.00

HOBBIES

____BLACKSTONE'S SECRETS OF MAGIC Harry Blackstone	2.00
____COIN COLLECTING FOR BEGINNERS Burton Hobson & Fred Reinfeld	2.00
____400 FASCINATING MAGIC TRICKS YOU CAN DO Howard Thurston	2.00
____GOULD'S GOLD & SILVER GUIDE TO COINS Maurice Gould	2.00
____HARMONICA PLAYING FOR FUN & PROFIT Hal Leighton	2.00
____HOW I TURN JUNK INTO FUN AND PROFIT Sari	3.00
____JUGGLING MADE EASY Rudolf Dittrich	2.00
____MAGIC MADE EASY Byron Wels	2.00
____SEW SIMPLY, SEW RIGHT Mini Rhea & F. Leighton	2.00
____STAMP COLLECTING FOR BEGINNERS Burton Hobson	2.00
____STAMP COLLECTING FOR FUN & PROFIT Frank Cetin	1.00

HORSE PLAYERS' WINNING GUIDES

____BETTING HORSES TO WIN Les Conklin	2.00
____HOW TO PICK WINNING HORSES Bob McKnight	2.00
____HOW TO WIN AT THE RACES Sam (The Genius) Lewin	2.00
____HOW YOU CAN BEAT THE RACES Jack Kavanagh	2.00

Melvin Powers SELF-IMPROVEMENT LIBRARY

____MAKING MONEY AT THE RACES David Barr	2.00
____PAYDAY AT THE RACES Les Conklin	2.00
____SMART HANDICAPPING MADE EASY William Bauman	2.00

HYPNOTISM

____ADVANCED TECHNIQUES OF HYPNOSIS Melvin Powers	1.00
____ANIMAL HYPNOSIS Dr. F. A. Völgyesi	2.00
____CHILDBIRTH WITH HYPNOSIS William S. Kroger, M.D.	2.00
____HOW TO SOLVE YOUR SEX PROBLEMS WITH SELF-HYPNOSIS Frank S. Caprio, M.D.	2.00
____HOW TO STOP SMOKING THRU SELF-HYPNOSIS Leslie M. LeCron	2.00
____HOW TO USE AUTO-SUGGESTION EFFECTIVELY John Duckworth	2.00
____HOW YOU CAN BOWL BETTER USING SELF-HYPNOSIS Jack Heise	2.00
____HOW YOU CAN PLAY BETTER GOLF USING SELF-HYPNOSIS Heise	2.00
____HYPNOSIS AND SELF-HYPNOSIS Bernard Hollander, M.D.	2.00
____HYPNOSIS IN ATHLETICS Wilfred M. Mitchell, Ph.D.	2.00
____HYPNOTISM (Originally published in 1893) Carl Sextus	3.00
____HYPNOTISM & PSYCHIC PHENOMENA Simeon Edmunds	2.00
____HYPNOTISM MADE EASY Dr. Ralph Winn	2.00
____HYPNOTISM MADE PRACTICAL Louis Orton	2.00
____HYPNOTISM REVEALED Melvin Powers	1.00
____HYPNOTISM TODAY Leslie LeCron & Jean Bordeaux, Ph.D.	2.00
____HYPNOTIST'S CASE BOOK Alex Erskine	1.00
____MEDICAL HYPNOSIS HANDBOOK Drs. Van Pelt, Ambrose, Newbold	2.00
____MODERN HYPNOSIS Lesley Kuhn & Salvatore Russo, Ph.D.	3.00
____NEW CONCEPTS OF HYPNOSIS Bernard C. Gindes, M.D.	3.00
____POST-HYPNOTIC INSTRUCTIONS Arnold Furst How to give post-hypnotic suggestions for therapeutic purposes.	2.00
____PRACTICAL GUIDE TO SELF-HYPNOSIS Melvin Powers	2.00
____PRACTICAL HYPNOTISM Philip Magonet, M.D.	1.00
____SECRETS OF HYPNOTISM S. J. Van Pelt, M.D.	2.00
____SELF-HYPNOSIS Paul Adams	2.00
____SELF-HYPNOSIS Its Theory, Technique & Application Melvin Powers	2.00
____SELF-HYPNOSIS A Conditioned-Response Technique Laurance Sparks	2.00
____THERAPY THROUGH HYPNOSIS edited by Raphael H. Rhodes	3.00

JUDAICA

____HOW TO LIVE A RICHER & FULLER LIFE Rabbi Edgar F. Magnin	2.00
____MODERN ISRAEL Lily Edelman	2.00
____OUR JEWISH HERITAGE Rabbi Alfred Wolf & Joseph Gaer	2.00
____ROMANCE OF HASSIDISM Jacob S. Minkin	2.50
____SERVICE OF THE HEART Evelyn Garfield, Ph.D.	2.50
____STORY OF ISRAEL IN COINS Jean & Maurice Gould	2.00
____STORY OF ISRAEL IN STAMPS Maxim & Gabriel Shamir	1.00
____TONGUE OF THE PROPHETS Robert St. John	3.00
____TREASURY OF COMFORT edited by Rabbi Sidney Greenberg	2.00

MARRIAGE, SEX & PARENTHOOD

____ABILITY TO LOVE Dr. Allan Fromme	3.00
____ENCYCLOPEDIA OF MODERN SEX & LOVE TECHNIQUES Macandrew	2.00

Melvin Powers SELF-IMPROVEMENT LIBRARY

	GUIDE TO SUCCESSFUL MARRIAGE *Drs. Albert Ellis & Robert Harper*	3.00
	HOW TO RAISE AN EMOTIONALLY HEALTHY, HAPPY CHILD, *A. Ellis*	2.00
	IMPOTENCE & FRIGIDITY *Edwin W. Hirsch, M.D.*	2.00
	NEW APPROACHES TO SEX IN MARRIAGE *John E. Eichenlaub, M.D.*	2.00
	PSYCHOSOMATIC GYNECOLOGY *William S. Kroger, M.D.*	10.00
	SEX WITHOUT GUILT *Albert Ellis, Ph.D.*	2.00
	SEXUALLY ADEQUATE FEMALE *Frank S. Caprio, M.D.*	2.00
	SEXUALLY ADEQUATE MALE *Frank S. Caprio, M.D.*	2.00
	YOUR FIRST YEAR OF MARRIAGE *Dr. Tom McGinnis*	2.00

METAPHYSICS & OCCULT

	BOOK OF TALISMANS, AMULETS & ZODIACAL GEMS *William Pavitt*	3.00
	CONCENTRATION—A Guide to Mental Mastery *Mouni Sadhu*	2.00
	DREAMS & OMENS REVEALED *Fred Gettings*	2.00
	EXTRASENSORY PERCEPTION *Simeon Edmunds*	2.00
	FORTUNE TELLING WITH CARDS *P. Foli*	2.00
	HANDWRITING ANALYSIS MADE EASY *John Marley*	2.00
	HANDWRITING TELLS *Nadya Olyanova*	3.00
	HOW TO UNDERSTAND YOUR DREAMS *Geoffrey A. Dudley*	2.00
	ILLUSTRATED YOGA *William Zorn*	2.00
	IN DAYS OF GREAT PEACE *Mouni Sadhu*	2.00
	KING SOLOMON'S TEMPLE IN THE MASONIC TRADITION *Alex Horne*	5.00
	MAGICIAN — His training and work *W. E. Butler*	2.00
	MEDITATION *Mouni Sadhu*	3.00
	MODERN NUMEROLOGY *Morris C. Goodman*	2.00
	NUMEROLOGY—ITS FACTS AND SECRETS *Ariel Yvon Taylor*	2.00
	PALMISTRY MADE EASY *Fred Gettings*	2.00
	PALMISTRY MADE PRACTICAL *Elizabeth Daniels Squire*	2.00
	PALMISTRY SECRETS REVEALED *Henry Frith*	2.00
	PRACTICAL YOGA *Ernest Wood*	2.00
	PROPHECY IN OUR TIME *Martin Ebon*	2.50
	PSYCHOLOGY OF HANDWRITING *Nadya Olyanova*	2.00
	SEEING INTO THE FUTURE *Harvey Day*	2.00
	SEX & HUMAN BEHAVIOR BY THE NUMBERS *Alexandra Kayhle*	2.00
	SUPERSTITION — Are you superstitious? *Eric Maple*	2.00
	TAROT *Mouni Sadhu*	4.00
	TAROT OF THE BOHEMIANS *Papus*	3.00
	TEST YOUR ESP *Martin Ebon*	2.00
	WAYS TO SELF-REALIZATION *Mouni Sadhu*	2.00
	WITCHCRAFT, MAGIC & OCCULTISM—A Fascinating History *W. B. Crow*	3.00
	WITCHCRAFT — THE SIXTH SENSE *Justine Glass*	2.00
	WORLD OF PSYCHIC RESEARCH *Hereward Carrington*	2.00
	YOU CAN ANALYZE HANDWRITING *Robert Holder*	2.00

SELF-HELP & INSPIRATIONAL

	ACT YOUR WAY TO SUCCESSFUL LIVING *Neil & Margaret Rau*	2.00
	CYBERNETICS WITHIN US *Y. Saparina*	3.00
	DOCTOR PSYCHO-CYBERNETICS *Maxwell Maltz, M.D.*	3.00
	DYNAMIC THINKING *Melvin Powers*	1.00

	GREATEST POWER IN THE UNIVERSE *U. S. Andersen*	4.00
	GROW RICH WHILE YOU SLEEP *Ben Sweetland*	2.00
	GROWTH THROUGH REASON *Albert Ellis, Ph.D.*	3.00
	GUIDE TO DEVELOPING YOUR POTENTIAL *Herbert A. Otto, Ph.D.*	3.00
	GUIDE TO HAPPINESS *Dr. Maxwell S. Cagan*	2.00
	GUIDE TO LIVING IN BALANCE *Frank S. Caprio, M.D.*	2.00
	GUIDE TO RATIONAL LIVING *Albert Ellis, Ph.D. & R. Harper, Ph.D.*	2.00
	HELPING YOURSELF WITH APPLIED PSYCHOLOGY *R. Henderson*	2.00
	HELPING YOURSELF WITH PSYCHIATRY *Frank S. Caprio, M.D.*	2.00
	HOW TO ATTRACT GOOD LUCK *A. H. Z. Carr*	2.00
	HOW TO CONTROL YOUR DESTINY *Norvell*	2.00
	HOW TO DEVELOP A WINNING PERSONALITY *Martin Panzer*	2.00
	HOW TO DEVELOP AN EXCEPTIONAL MEMORY *Young & Gibson*	3.00
	HOW TO OVERCOME YOUR FEARS *M. P. Leahy, M.D.*	2.00
	HOW YOU CAN HAVE CONFIDENCE AND POWER *Les Giblin*	2.00
	I WILL *Ben Sweetland*	2.00
	LEFT-HANDED PEOPLE *Michael Barsley*	3.00
	MAGIC IN YOUR MIND *U. S. Andersen*	2.00
	MAGIC OF THINKING BIG *Dr. David J. Schwartz*	2.00
	MAGIC POWER OF YOUR MIND *Walter M. Germain*	3.00
	MASTER KEYS TO SUCCESS, POPULARITY & PRESTIGE *C. W. Bailey*	2.00
	MENTAL POWER THRU SLEEP SUGGESTION *Melvin Powers*	1.00
	ORIENTAL SECRETS OF GRACEFUL LIVING *Boye De Mente*	1.00
	PSYCHO-CYBERNETICS *Maxwell Maltz, M.D.*	2.00
	SECRET OF SECRETS *U. S. Andersen*	3.00
	SELF-CONFIDENCE THROUGH SELF-ANALYSIS *E. Oakley*	1.00
	STUTTERING AND WHAT YOU CAN DO ABOUT IT *W. Johnson, Ph.D.*	2.00
	SUCCESS-CYBERNETICS *U. S. Andersen*	2.00
	10 DAYS TO A GREAT NEW LIFE *William E. Edwards*	2.00
	THINK AND GROW RICH *Napoleon Hill*	2.00
	THREE MAGIC WORDS *U. S. Andersen*	3.00
	TREASURY OF THE ART OF LIVING edited by *Rabbi S. Greenberg*	2.00
	YOU ARE NOT THE TARGET *Laura Huxley*	3.00
	YOUR SUBCONSCIOUS POWER *Charles M. Simmons*	2.00
	YOUR THOUGHTS CAN CHANGE YOUR LIFE *Donald Curtis*	2.00

SPORTS

	ARCHERY — An Expert's Guide *Don Stamp*	2.00
	BICYCLING FOR FUN AND GOOD HEALTH *Kenneth E. Luther*	2.00
	COMPLETE GUIDE TO FISHING *Vlad Evanoff*	2.00
	HOW TO BEAT BETTER TENNIS PLAYERS *Loring Fiske*	3.00
	HOW TO WIN AT POCKET BILLIARDS *Edward D. Knuchell*	3.00
	HOW TO WIN AT THE RACES *Sam (The Genius) Lewin*	2.00
	MOTORCYCLING FOR BEGINNERS *I. G. Edmonds*	2.00
	PRACTICAL BOATING *W. S. Kals*	3.00
	PSYCH YOURSELF TO BETTER TENNIS *Dr. Walter A. Luszki*	2.00
	SECRET OF BOWLING STRIKES *Dawson Taylor*	2.00
	SECRET OF PERFECT PUTTING *Horton Smith & Dawson Taylor*	2.00
	SECRET WHY FISH BITE *James Westman*	2.00
	SKIER'S POCKET BOOK *Otti Wiedman* (4¼" x 6")	2.50
	TABLE TENNIS MADE EASY *Johnny Leach*	2.00
	TENNIS FOR BEGINNERS *Dr. H. A. Murray*	2.00
	TENNIS MADE EASY *Joel Brecheen*	2.00

WILSHIRE MINIATURE LIBRARY (4¼" x 6" in full color)

	BUTTERFLIES	2.50
	INTRODUCTION TO MINERALS	2.50
	LIPIZZANERS & THE SPANISH RIDING SCHOOL	2.50
	PRECIOUS STONES AND PEARLS	2.50
	SKIER'S POCKET BOOK	2.50

WILSHIRE HORSE LOVERS' LIBRARY

AMATEUR HORSE BREEDER *A. C. Leighton Hardman*	2.00
AMERICAN QUARTER HORSE IN PICTURES *Margaret Cabell Self*	2.00
APPALOOSA HORSE *Bill & Dona Richardson*	2.00
ARABIAN HORSE *Reginald S. Summerhays*	2.00
ART OF WESTERN RIDING *Suzanne Norton Jones*	2.00
AT THE HORSE SHOW *Margaret Cabell Self*	2.00
BACK-YARD FOAL *Peggy Jett Pittinger*	2.00
BACK-YARD HORSE *Peggy Jett Pittinger*	2.00
BASIC DRESSAGE *Jean Froissard*	2.00
BEGINNER'S GUIDE TO THE WESTERN HORSE *Natlee Kenoyer*	2.00
BITS—THEIR HISTORY, USE AND MISUSE *Louis Taylor*	2.00
BLOND GIRL WITH BLUE EYES LEADING PALOMINO (Full color poster 47" x 27")	5.00
BREAKING & TRAINING THE DRIVING HORSE *Doris Ganton*	2.00
CAVALRY MANUAL OF HORSEMANSHIP *Gordon Wright*	2.00
COMPLETE TRAINING OF HORSE AND RIDER *Colonel Alois Podhajsky*	3.00
DOG TRAINING MADE EASY & FUN *John W. Kellogg*	2.00
DRESSAGE—A study of the Finer Points in Riding *Henry Wynmalen*	3.00
DRIVING HORSES *Sallie Walrond*	2.00
EQUITATION *Jean Froissard*	3.00
FIRST AID FOR HORSES *Dr. Charles H. Denning, Jr.*	2.00
FUN OF RAISING A COLT *Rubye & Frank Griffith*	2.00
FUN ON HORSEBACK *Margaret Cabell Self*	3.00
HORSE OWNER'S CONCISE GUIDE *Elsie V. Hanauer*	2.00
HORSE SELECTION & CARE FOR BEGINNERS *George H. Conn*	2.00
HORSE SENSE—A complete guide to riding and care *Alan Deacon*	4.00
HORSEBACK RIDING FOR BEGINNERS *Louis Taylor*	3.00
HORSEBACK RIDING MADE EASY & FUN *Sue Henderson Coen*	2.00
HORSES—Their Selection, Care & Handling *Margaret Cabell Self*	2.00
HOW TO WIN AT THE RACES *Sam (The Genius) Lewin*	2.00
HUNTER IN PICTURES *Margaret Cabell Self*	2.00
ILLUSTRATED BOOK OF THE HORSE *S. Sidney* (8½" x 11½")	10.00
ILLUSTRATED HORSE MANAGEMENT—400 Illustrations *Dr. E. Mayhew*	5.00
ILLUSTRATED HORSE TRAINING *Captain M. H. Hayes*	5.00
ILLUSTRATED HORSEBACK RIDING FOR BEGINNERS *Jeanne Mellin*	2.00
JUMPING—Learning and Teaching *Jean Froissard*	2.00
LIPIZZANERS & THE SPANISH RIDING SCHOOL *W. Reuter* (4¼" x 6")	2.50
MORGAN HORSE IN PICTURES *Margaret Cabell Self*	2.00
MOVIE HORSES—The Fascinating Techniques of Training *Anthony Amaral*	2.00
POLICE HORSES *Judith Campbell*	2.00
PRACTICAL GUIDE TO HORSESHOEING	2.00
PRACTICAL HORSE PSYCHOLOGY *Moyra Williams*	2.00
PROBLEM HORSES *Reginald S. Summerhays* Tested Guide for Curing Most Common & Serious Horse Behavior Habits	2.00
RESCHOOLING THE THOROUGHBRED *Peggy Jett Pittinger*	2.00
RIDE WESTERN *Louis Taylor*	2.00
SCHOOLING YOUR YOUNG HORSE *George Wheatley*	2.00
STABLE MANAGEMENT FOR THE OWNER-GROOM *George Wheatley*	3.00
TEACHING YOUR HORSE TO JUMP *W. J. Froud*	2.00
THE LAW AND YOUR HORSE *Edward H. Greene*	3.00
TRAIL HORSES & TRAIL RIDING *Anne & Perry Westbrook*	2.00
TREATING COMMON DISEASES OF YOUR HORSE *Dr. George H. Conn*	2.00
TREATING HORSE AILMENTS *G. W. Serth*	2.00
WONDERFUL WORLD OF PONIES *Peggy Jett Pittinger* (8½" x 11½")	4.00
YOUR FIRST HORSE *George C. Saunders, M.D.*	**2.00**
YOUR PONY BOOK *Hermann Wiederhold*	2.00
YOUR WESTERN HORSE *Nelson C. Nye*	2.00

The books listed above can be obtained from your book dealer or directly from Wilshire Book Company. When ordering, please remit 25c per book postage & handling. Send one dollar for our 224 page illustrated catalog of self-improvement books.
Wilshire Book Company, 12015 Sherman Road, No. Hollywood, California 91605

NOTES

NOTES

NOTES

NOTES

NOTES

NOTES

NOTES

NOTES

NOTES

NOTES

NOTES